SETHY I
KING OF EGYPT

SETHY I
KING OF EGYPT

HIS LIFE AND AFTERLIFE

AIDAN DODSON

The American University in Cairo Press
Cairo   New York

First published in 2019 by
The American University in Cairo Press
113 Sharia Kasr el Aini, Cairo, Egypt
200 Park Ave., Suite 1700, New York, NY 10166
www.aucpress.com

Dar el Kutub No. 27483/17
ISBN 978 977 416 886 4

Dar el Kutub Cataloging-in-Publication Data

Dodson, Aidan
    Sethy I, King of Egypt: His Life and Afterlife / Aidan Dodson.—
Cairo: The American University in Cairo Press, 2019.
        p.cm.
        ISBN 978 977 416 886 4
        1. Egypt—Antiquities
        932

1 2 3 4 5   23 22 21 20 19

Designed by Carolyn Gibson
Printed in China

To the memory of my mother, Edna Dodson, née Clark,
1926–2017

CONTENTS

PREFACE   ix

INTRODUCTION   1

ABBREVIATIONS AND CONVENTIONS   3

1   THE CRADLE OF SETHY I   5

2   THE REIGN OF SETHY I   17

3   THE MANSION OF MILLIONS OF YEARS   69
    AND THE HOUSE OF ETERNITY

4   LIMBO   115

5   RESURRECTION   119

CHRONOLOGY   159

NOTES   161

BIBLIOGRAPHY   169

SOURCES OF IMAGES   179

INDEX   181

PREFACE

The origins of this book go back to a question posed to a leading Egyptian bookseller as to whether there was any particular book he was regularly asked for—but that didn't currently exist. The response was "Something on Sethy I and his tomb." This is that book!

A hint that I might be the person to write such a volume was willingly accepted since the topic represents a nexus between a number of my research interests: the political history of ancient Egypt, its funerary architecture, the history of archaeology in Egypt, and the ancient culture's reception into modern consciousness. Apropos the first of these, I had already written books on the second half of the Eighteenth Dynasty as well as on the second half of the Nineteenth; accordingly, something involving part of the intervening eight decades seemed attractive, while the tomb of Sethy I represented a major milestone in the evolution of the Egyptian royal tomb. Finally, the discovery of that tomb and its subsequent presentation was a key event in the absorption of ancient Egypt into modern British (and wider) culture—not to mention the subsequent fate of the tomb as a case study (and warning) regarding the postdiscovery conservation of such a monument.

Accordingly, this book aims to tell the story of Sethy I from the events that led to his family's assumption of the throne of Egypt during the fourteenth century BC, through his reign, death, burial, and reburial, to his nineteenth century AD rediscovery and ongoing research into the twenty-first century. In doing so, I have attempted to tell the tale in an accessible way while also making the volume of use to scholars—hence the extensive endnotes and bibliography.

I have been able to keep these latter to a manageable size, and have been greatly aided in the process of research and writing by the existence of three works: my old teacher Ken Kitchen's seminal *Ramesside Inscriptions* series, a superhuman piece of work that makes all the key texts of the period available in both transcription and translation (with ongoing commentary volumes); the lamented Bill Murnane's *Road to Kadesh*, which provides a magisterial analysis of Sethy I's foreign policy; and his student Peter Brand's fine doctoral dissertation, *The Monuments of Seti I*. Between them they have provided the vast majority of the underlying data and discussions of the period. Ken's and Peter's works provide a comprehensive bibliography for the monuments and documents they cover, with references to other material provided primarily through the lens of Porter and Moss's *Topographical Bibliography* volumes. Accordingly, most of my references are to these works, although where substantive treatments have appeared since the relevant work closed for press, these have also been cited.

As always, many individuals deserve my particular gratitude for a wide range of kindnesses: Taher Aboudi, Magdi Abu-Hamid Ali, Bernardette Brady, Peter Brand, Peter Clayton, Rosario Cornejo, Sue Giles, Salima Ikram, Adam Lowe, Stephanie Moser, John Taylor, and Kent R. Weeks. As always, my wife, Dyan Hilton, deserves my thanks for proofreading and continuing to put up with me. Finally, I must acknowledge the decades of support given to me by my late mother, who died while this book was being written and to whose memory it is dedicated.

INTRODUCTION

 King Sethy I ruled Egypt for a decade during the first part of the thirteenth century BC. His era fell during one of the best-known and most prosperous periods of the history of the eastern Mediterranean and Near East—the Late Bronze Age. During this period the Egyptian empire had reached its zenith, stretching from northern Syria to deep in Upper Nubia, Egypt interacting both militarily and diplomatically with many of the other great powers of her time, and grown rich on trade and plunder. However, this golden age was approaching its end, and little over a century later the world would collapse into a dark age, with Egypt in a decline from which she would never fully recover.

Nevertheless, this was still beyond the horizon when Sethy's family found itself on the Egyptian throne after a series of kings had failed to leave a blood heir; indeed, it may have been the very existence of Sethy and his young son, the future Rameses II, that cemented his father Rameses I's candidacy for the throne of the pharaohs. On the other hand, Egyptian culture had recently emerged from a major upheaval in the form of the short-lived religious revolution of Akhenaten, which had seen the ancient gods sidelined in favor of a new form of sun worship, accompanied by an ideological and physical distortion of art forms, all of which would have a lasting effect on the country's future.

Thus, the counterreformation that had begun soon after Akhenaten's death had restored the old religious structure, yet things had by no means reverted to the status quo ante, with many aspects of art, architecture, and implicitly, the nature of the state, shifting during the transition back. The death of the last of a royal line that stretched back centuries had brought commoners—albeit royally connected commoners—to the throne, their mutual profession of soldier underlining the martial theme that had underpinned the Egyptian state since the expulsion of the Hyksos occupiers by the kings of Thebes over three centuries earlier.

Thus, the role of military leader was one to which all monarchs of the Egyptian New Kingdom aspired, whether manifested in a lifetime on the battlefield (Thutmose III) or a need to paint large local police actions (Amenhotep III). When Sethy I came to the throne this role for the king was a real one, as Egypt's possessions and vassals in northern Syria were under steady pressure from an expansive Hittite empire, exacerbated by

FIGURE 1 Statuette of Sethy I, dating to the later years of his reign; from either Abydos or Karnak, Mut temple (Cairo CG751).

a deeper hostility caused by unfortunate events that had followed the death of Tutankhamun, the last of the old royal line, some years earlier. Accordingly, Sethy would fight the Hittites and their allies in a continuum of campaigns that would continue into the reign of Rameses II, until at length the two powers made peace.

Post-Akhenaten mores also seem to have led to a growth in outward shows of piety on the part of the king, with Sethy undertaking major works for the gods, also being shown striking a much more humble pose before the gods than had many of his predecessors. These works were carried out in an exquisite style that was distinctive of his reign, which is often held to be an apex of Egyptian art, and perhaps a barometer of the personal tastes of Sethy himself. Among such monuments was his tomb, decorated on a scale never before seen and the discovery of which in the early nineteenth century AD was an epoch-making event in the modern discovery and reception of ancient Egypt in the West.

The story of Sethy I, his life and monuments, and their rediscovery thus covers a range of important themes within Egyptology. Accordingly, this book aims to weave them together into a narrative that spans over some three and a half millennia, beginning with the Egypt into which he was born and what has been learned and surmised about his origins and early life. We then move on to his career as king, both as a restorer and builder and also as a military leader. His funerary monuments are given special treatment as providing the backdrop to an 'afterlife' that featured the robbery and multiple reburials of his mummy, and then—after a hiatus of millennia—the modern discovery of that mummy and the king's monuments, a story that is still certainly not yet complete.

ABBREVIATIONS AND CONVENTIONS

BibNat	Bibliothèque Nationale, Paris, France.
BM	British Museum, London, UK.
Bristol	Bristol City Museum & Art Gallery, Bristol, UK.
Brooklyn	Brooklyn Museum, New York, USA.
Brussels	Musées royaux d'Art et d'Histoire, Brussels, Belgium.
Cairo	Egyptian Museum, Cairo, Egypt.
Chicago	Oriental Institute Museum, University of Chicago, USA.
Florence	Museo Archeologico, Florence, Italy.
Istanbul	Eski Şark Eserleri Müzesi, Istanbul, Turkey.
Khartoum	Sudan National Museum, Khartoum, Sudan.
LPH	Life, Prosperity, & Health (ancient wish).
Louvre	Musée du Louvre, Paris, France.
MMA	Metropolitan Museum of Art, New York, USA.
Munich	Staatliche Museum Ägyptischer Kunst, Munich, Germany.
Rockefeller	Rockefeller Museum, East Jerusalem.
Soane	Sir John Soane's Museum, London, UK.
Turin	Museo Egizio, Turin, Italy.
Vatican	Museo Gregoriano Egizio, Vatican.

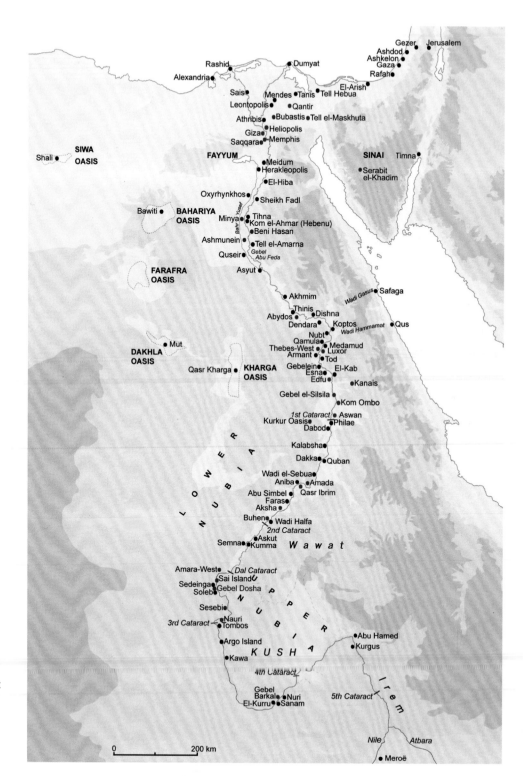

FIGURE 2
Egypt and
Nubia: sites
with significant
material from
the reign of
Sethy I are
marked
in red.

1 THE CRADLE OF SETHY I

FIGURE 3 The Near East during the time of Sethy I: principal sites relating to the reign of Sethy I are marked in red.

The family of Sethy I came to the throne of Egypt following the extinction of the royal house of the Eighteenth Dynasty, which traced its origins back into at least the middle of the sixteenth century BC, when Kamose and Ahmose I had liberated Egypt from the Palestinian Hyksos occupiers. Subsequently, Thutmose I and his grandson Thutmose III had carved out an Egyptian empire, stretching from northern Syria to Upper Nubia (modern northern Sudan), meaning that by the fourteenth century, Egypt, further enriched by the extensive gold mines of the Eastern Desert and Nubia, was at the peak of her wealth and international influence. As a manifestation of the latter, the king of Egypt was one of the era's 'great powers,' whose rulers corresponded with each other on equal terms and called one another 'brother.'[1]

However, the middle of the century saw an upheaval in Egypt when King Amenhotep IV, soon to rename himself Akhenaten, brought to prominence a new incarnation of the sun god, who soon

FIGURE 4 Section of balustrade showing Akhenaten, Nefertiti, and their eldest daughter, Meryetaten, worshiping the Aten, carved in the extreme style of the earlier part of the reign; from Amarna (Cairo TR 30/10/26/12).

advanced to become the predominant god of Egypt (fig. 4), with the ancient deities eclipsed and their cults apparently starved of resources.[2] Things were taken a step further with Amun-Re, 'King of the Gods,' whose claims to divine overlordship were countered by his names and images being erased wherever found. That the revolution was political as well as theological was demonstrated by the foundation of a new capital city at Amarna, halfway between the old centers of Memphis and Thebes.

Nevertheless, as soon as Akhenaten was dead, an accommodation between the old and new was attempted early in the reign of Akhenaten's young successor, Tutankhaten, probably under the direction of the late king's female coregent, Neferneferuaten, all but certainly none other than his wife, Nefertiti. However, with her disappearance three years after Akhenaten's death, a more comprehensive counterreformation and restoration of monuments damaged under Akhenaten was instituted under a new regent, the general Horemheb, and the king (still not yet into his teens) renamed Tutankhamun. His wife, Akhenaten's third daughter, Ankhesenpaaten, was also renamed for Amun.

Little more than a half-decade later, Tutankhamun was dead at eighteen with no known living children.[3] The throne was taken by another general, Ay (fig. 6), possibly the late king's maternal grandfather, but only after an interregnum during which the dowager queen Ankhesenamun attempted to marry a Hittite prince and make him king. The 'Hittite candidate' was killed during this episode, the Hittite king blaming the Egyptian authorities for his demise. Whether he was correct to do so remains unknown, but this perception by the Hittites would sour Egypto–Hittite relations for decades to come.

On Ay's death, Horemheb became king, Ay's only known son, Nakhtmin, having either predeceased him or died in what may have

FIGURE 5 Ay carrying out the Opening of the Mouth ritual at the funeral of Tutankhamun; this is the only case in a royal tomb where the officiant is explicitly the king's successor; KV62.

FIGURE 6 Horemheb offering to Amun-Re; gateway of Pylon X at Karnak.

been a power struggle. The new king continued the policy begun under Tutankhamun of religious restoration and reform, being responsible for a considerable amount of building at the great Amun temple at Karnak and elsewhere (fig. 5). However, he had no surviving son by his only known wife,[4] Mutnedjmet (possibly the sister of Nefertiti of that name), and thus needed to make other arrangements for the royal succession.

While no formal statement of the laws of succession to the Egyptian throne survives, it can be inferred from circumstantial evidence that the heir to the throne should be the eldest son of the king (ideally by his Great Wife), who would at some point be formally proclaimed heir and would eventually carry out his father's burial as the final act of a dutiful son to his father. Where no blood son survived, it would appear that another could be proclaimed as heir, and that in the absence of such a proclamation, the person who took the son's place in the funeral ceremonies would be the legitimate heir. The latter may have been Ay's legal basis for succeeding Tutankhamun, possibly explaining his unique depiction carrying out the Opening of the Mouth ceremony in Tutankhamun's tomb.

As his heir, Horemheb chose an old army colleague, General Paramessu, who was also serving as his vizier, two scribal statues of whom were found just inside the gateway of Pylon X at Karnak (fig. 7).[5] From these we learn that he was also 'Deputy of his Person in Upper and Lower Egypt' and 'Noble in the Entire Land.' These titles closely mirror those held by Horemheb himself as regent during Tutankhamun's reign, and it is clear that these latter titles are to be understood as marking him out as the heir to the

FIGURE 7 Paramessu as vizier of Horemheb; from Karnak, gateway of Pylon X (Cairo JE44861).

throne. Paramessu was also 'Overseer of the Priests of All the Gods,' a title very similar to one once held by Thutmose B, the elder brother of Akhenaten, as original heir to Amenhotep III.

The statues also state that Paramessu was the son of a Troop Commander and Judge, Sethy (A).[6] The latter's tomb stela survives (naming him as 'Suty,' a well-attested variant of 'Sethy,' avoiding the use of the sometimes-problematic figure of the god Seth: cf. page 18),[7] including representations of a brother named Khaemwaset (B), who was a fan-bearer of the retinue, and an individual whose filiation is lost but who is named as Stable Master Ramose (fig. 8).[8] It would seem most likely that the latter was Sethy's son and that he was none other than Paramessu at the beginning of his career, the two names being fundamentally the same, the optional nature of 'Pa' being shown by its being dropped when Paramessu became king, while the terminal -sw was also used only intermittently by (and for) Paramessu once he had become Rameses I. Another early attestation of Paramessu/Ramose may be in the person of the Scribe of the Army, Ramose, who appears as Horemheb's adjutant in the tomb, the latter constructed at Saqqara during the reign of Tutankhamun.[9]

It is possible that Sethy A was the Egyptian envoy 'Shuta/Shutta' mentioned as active in Mesopotamia and Syria-Palestine during the reigns of Amenhotep III and Akhenaten,[10] but unlike Paramessu he is not attested with the actual title of Royal Envoy. Another possible identification is of a fan-bearer on the right of the king, Khaemwaset, known from a statue from Kawa, with Khaemwaset B;[11] if correct, the latter's wife will have been one Taemwadjsy, who was Head of the Harem of Tutankhamun, thus dating this phase of his career.

The material relating to Sethy A says nothing about the family's origins, but the compounding of his name with that of the god Seth, a relatively uncommon occurrence before his descendants' ascent to the throne, would suggest that they came from one of the centers of that god's worship. The principal ones were at Ombos in Upper Egypt and Tell el-Daba (Avaris) in the northeastern Delta,[12] the latter more likely, given the favor the Nineteenth Dynasty kings later showed the region, where their principal residence would soon be established (see page 28).

This idea is further reinforced by a stela carved under Rameses II, but referring back to an earlier time. Known as the Year 400 Stela (fig. 9),[13] this records some kind of quadricentenary relating to the god Seth that had in the past been celebrated by a

> Noble, Mayor of the City and Vizier, Fan-Bearer on the Right of the King, Troop Commander, Overseer of Foreign Countries, Overseer of the Fortress of Tjel, Chief of Police, Royal Scribe, Master of Horse, Conductor of the Feast of the Ram-the-Lord-of-Mendes, high priest of Seth, Lector-priest of Wadjet-She-Who-Opens-the-Two-Lands

FIGURE 8 Fragment of a stela of the father of Rameses I, Sethy A, who is shown in the center, flanked by an unidentified man and a woman. On the left, "his beloved brother," Khaemwaset, makes an offering, while on the right is Stable Master Ramose—probably Sethy's son, the later Rameses I (Chicago 11456).

and Overseer of the Prophets of All the Gods, Sethy, the Son of the Noble, Mayor of the City and Vizier, Troop Commander, Overseer of Foreign Countries, Overseer of the Fortress of Tjel, Royal Scribe and Master of Horse, Paramose, the Triumphant, Born of the Lady of the House and Singer of the Pre, Tia.

Although the terminology of the stela is somewhat obscure, its implication seems to be that the vizier Sethy was none other than the future Sethy I, further reinforced by the name and titles of his father (apparently the future Rameses I).

Against this identification is the fact that Sethy I's mother seems to have been named Sitre: a statue of a King's Great Wife Sitre is shown standing behind ones of Rameses I and Sethy I in the latter's Abydos temple and is also named in Sethy's tomb as part of the Opening of the Mouth sequence of scenes. In addition, a King's Great Wife and King's Mother Sitre-owned tomb, QV38 in the Valley of the Queens, stylistically can only date to the very end of the Eighteenth or the very beginning of the Nineteenth Dynasty.

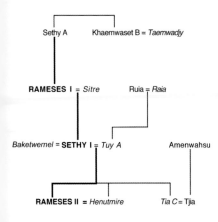

Rameses I's wife was unequivocally shown in a scene from a chapel at Abydos commemorating Rameses I (fig. 10; see page 31), but her name is now lost. The solution is probably that just as Paramessu revised his name when he became king, Tia changed or compounded hers on becoming queen. Tia was certainly a name known in the family of Sethy I, as implied by the fact that one of his daughters was given just this name (see pages 18–19). On this basis, it seems likely that Paramessu was joined in the vizierate by his son Sethy toward the end of Horemheb's reign, perhaps as the northern vizier while his father held the southern post (the vizierate had been split during the Eighteenth Dynasty into two regional offices).

In the aforementioned Abydos chapel, Rameses I and his wife were originally followed by three males and five females, but unfortunately all names and titles are lost, apart from damaged traces in the case of two of the women, making it unclear whether they represented Rameses I's parents, siblings, children, or a mixture of more than one group.[14] Thus, as the reign of Horemheb drew to an end, the destiny of Egypt was firmly in the hands of Paramessu and his son Sethy. Latest estimates of the latter's age at death place it between forty and fifty years (see page 149), making him in his thirties at the death of Horemheb. Depending on the view one takes concerning the ongoing debate

FIGURE 9 Scene at the top of the "Year 400 Stela"; Rameses II, with the "Vizier Sethy" (probably Sethy I) behind him, offers to the god Seth; from Tanis (Cairo JE6039).

FIGURE 10 Wall of the chapel of Rameses I at Abydos, showing on the right Rameses I and his wife offering to Osiris, and behind them various members of the king's family. Some parts of the scene could not be preserved and are represented by drawings made in situ (MMA 11.155.3c-d).

on the length of the latter's reign—the options seem to be fourteen years or double that[15]—Sethy would seem to have been born either during the latter years of Akhenaten or around the end of the reign of Tutankhamun.

To judge by the career of his own son, Sethy had by the last years of Horemheb become a father at least once, with his wife Tuy (later sometimes Muttuy), the daughter of the chariotry officer Raia and his wife Ruia (fig. 11). Sethy's marriage into another military family reinforces the picture of the military nature of the ruling elite of the late Eighteenth Dynasty, with a succession of professional soldiers following Tutankhamun on the Egyptian throne.

On Horemheb's death, Paramessu became king, but if indeed an old comrade of the late pharaoh, he is unlikely to have been much younger than him and was probably from the outset fairly dependent on his son and heir. In his cartouche names (cf. page 17), the new king clearly intended to link himself with the reunifier of Egypt at the end of the Second Intermediate Period and founder of the New Kingdom, Ahmose I. He thus employed a simplified form of his birth name as a nomen ('Rameses,' differing from that of Ahmose I only in the god invoked and an additional *s*), and a prenomen that differed from the earlier king in only one element (*Men*pehtyre versus *Neb*pehtyre):

the conscious nature of the latter is made clear by the fact that they were the *only* Egyptian kings *ever* to incorporate the *phty-* element.

Material from the reign of Rameses I is scarce, restricted to a few stelae (for example, fig. 13), architectural fragments, and a handful of reliefs in the gateway of Pylon II (built by Horemheb) at Karnak.[16] No contemporary document relates to Sethy in his new role as crown prince, although a retrospective account in the dedicatory stela from the Rameses I chapel at Abydos gives the following account of his princely career:

> My father began the kingship of Re, seated on the throne like him . . . . It was he, indeed
> who created my beauty; he made great my family in (people's) minds. He gave me his
> counsels as my safeguard, and his teaching was like a rampart in my heart . . . . I subdued
> for him the lands of the Fenkhu (a Levantine people), and I repulsed for him dissidents
> from the desert, (so that) I might protect Egypt for him as he wished, and I organized
> his kingship for him there . . . . I mustered his army and gave it unity of purpose. I sought
> out for him the condition of the Two Lands, and I wielded for him my strong arm as his
> bodyguard in foreign lands whose names were unknown. I was a valiant hero before him,
> so that he opened his eyes to my goodness.[17]

While it is thus clear that Sethy served as Rameses I's army commander and deputy, it has in the past been further speculated that Sethy might have become his father's formal coregent. However, there is no actual evidence for this, all juxtapositions of the two kings' names and images being memorializations of Rameses by his son (for example, his representations in the Hypostyle Hall at Karnak: see pages 47–48).[18]

FIGURE 11 The chariotry officer Raia and his wife Ruia, the parents-in-law of Sethy I, shown following their daughter Tuy on a block from the Ramesseum, later reused at Medinet Habu (Ramesseum).

In the event, Rameses's reign lasted for less than two years, his last record being dated to II *prt* 20 in Year 2, although as his accession date is unknown, it is not currently possible to calculate an absolute minimum length for his reign. As for when he died, III *šmw* 24 appears likely to have been the date of Sethy's accession in his place, so that Rameses will have outlived his last record by almost exactly five months.[19] After such a short reign, Rameses's building projects were all far from completion, including his tomb in the Valley of the Kings (KV16).[20] This was hurriedly made capable of receiving an interment, with a burial chamber enlarged out of what had been intended to be the beginning of a corridor, decorated in paint only rather than the laborious technique of painted raised relief introduced by Horemheb (see page 84), as was much of the king's great granite sarcophagus, only a few texts having been carved when news of the king's death came to the atelier (fig. 12). With the closure of the sarcophagus and tomb, the reign of Rameses I was over—and that of Sethy I formally begun.

FIGURE 12 The burial chamber of Rameses I in
KV16 in the Valley of the Kings; the decoration of the
sarcophagus was completed in paint, its carving having
been incomplete at the king's death.

FIGURE 13 Stela showing Rameses I offering to Seth;
from Tell Hebua (Cairo JE100012).

2 THE REIGN OF SETHY I

Beginnings

As with all Egyptian kings, Sethy I took a five-fold titulary on his accession. His 'basic' names ran as follows:

Horus

kꜣ-nḫt ḫꜥ m Wꜣst sꜥnḫ tꜣwy
Strong bull, who appears in Thebes and makes the Two Lands live

Nebti

wḥm-mswt sḫm-ḫpš dr pḏwt 9
Repeater of births, who repels the Nine Bows

Golden Falcon

wḥm ḫꜥw wsr-pḏwt m tꜣw nb
One who has repeated appearances, strong of troops in all lands

Prenomen

Mn-mꜣꜥt-Rꜥ
Establisher of the *maat* of Re

Nomen

Stẖy-mr-n-Ptḥ
The Sethian, beloved of Ptah

Until the middle of the Eighteenth Dynasty, all five names had been essentially fixed throughout a reign, with only a few minor exceptions. However, since the time of Thutmose III, the Horus, Nebti, and Golden Horus names had become much more mutable, with alternate versions used on occasion in place of the main formulations.

Some were variants of these 'basic' names, while others were wholly new, with versions occasionally specific to a given location.[1] In Sethy I's case, some thirty Horus names have been recorded, with seven Nebti and eight Golden Falcon names. His prenomina and nomina were far less variable, differing mainly as regards spelling and orthography, sometimes with the addition of an epithet to the prenomen. However, the vast majority of Sethy's prenomina remained 'basic.' The principal substantive variation in the king's nomen was to replace Ptah with Amun in the 'Merenptah' element in some places in the Hypostyle Hall of the temple of Amun-Re at Karnak, so giving 'Sethy-Merenamun.'

The most interesting variant orthography is found in examples of the nomen inscribed at Abydos and in the king's tomb in the Valley of the Kings. Here, the Seth-hieroglyph is replaced by a figure of Osiris, or sometimes the Osirian *tjet*-knot, clearly reflecting concerns over Seth's mythological status as the antagonist of Osiris, god of Abydos and of the dead, in such contexts. For similar reasons, other persons named Sethy frequently spelled out the god's name phonetically on funerary monuments—one example being the stela of the king's grandfather, Sethy A, who appears there as "Suty" (pages 9–10).

As noted in the previous chapter, Sethy I's father, Rameses I, had used his cartouche names to link himself back to the founder of Egypt's New Kingdom prosperity, Ahmose I. Such continuity can also be seen in Sethy's choice of prenomen, taking its *mn*-element from that of Rameses I, and combining it with the *m3't* that formed the core of the prenomen of Amenhotep III, the last orthodox king prior to the Amarna Period. It also, of course, linked him with the whole concept of cosmic order implicit in the concept of 'Maat.' The core of his Nebti name, *whm-mswt* (repeating of births), also had wide-ranging significance, not only proclaiming a "renaissance,"[2] but also reaching back in time to the Middle Kingdom, when Amenemhat I, founder of the Twelfth Dynasty,[3] had adopted *Whm-mswt* as his Horus name, clearly again laying claim to presiding over a period of renewal.

The Royal Family

Given that he was an adult when he succeeded his father a decade later, Prince Rameses A (later King Rameses II) had certainly been born well before Sethy I's accession. The situation is less clear as regards Rameses's sister Tia (C), as all our evidence regarding her comes from the reign of her brother, during which she was married to the overseer of treasurers Tjia, with whom she shared a tomb at Saqqara (fig. 14).[4]

Curiously, nothing appears to survive from Sethy's own reign, even mentioning his wife, Queen Tuy: all her attestations come from the reign of Rameses II.[5] Thus it is unclear whether her tomb, QV80 in the Valley of the Queens (fig. 15),[6] was begun under her husband or under her son. The tomb was considerably larger than Sitre's KV38,

FIGURE 14 The tomb of Sethy I's daughter Tia and son-in-law Tjia at Saqqara; directly to the right is the tomb of Horemheb, built prior to his accession to the throne.

comprising an antechamber, flanked by a pair of subsidiary rooms, preceding a stairway down to a four-pillared burial chamber, with three annexes, representing the most elaborate New Kingdom queen's sepulcher to date. The tomb is now in a very poor condition, and only a few fragments of decoration, in raised relief, survive, including at least one image of the queen; of her major funerary equipment, only the lid of one of her canopic jars has been recovered (fig. 16).

Tuy was certainly prominent during her son's reign, living until at least Rameses's Year 21, when she wrote to the king and queen of the Hittites as part of the correspondence surrounding the Egypto–Hittite treaty agreed between the two nations that year; a Year 22 docket, found on a fragment of wine jar in her tomb, might suggest her death soon afterward. Various statues were manufactured representing her, including a colossus in her son's memorial temple,[7] while she appeared in at least one relief in the same building (fig. 18), and as a subsidiary figure on a number of Rameses's own colossi. Queen

FIGURE 15 Valley of the Queens, with the locations of the tombs of Sethy I's mother, Sitre (QV38), wife Tuy (QV80), and his probable daughter, Henutmire (QV75), marked.

Tuy also featured in a now-fragmentary series of reliefs depicting her son's divine birth, originally on a wall of a chapel built alongside his memorial temple, the Ramesseum (fig. 17).[8]

In addition to Tuy, Sethy may have had another wife. A papyrus of the late Twentieth Dynasty records the robbery of the tomb, probably in the Valley of the Queens, of a "King's Wife Baketwernel of King Menmaatre."[9] Although the king at the time of the papyrus, Rameses XI, was a Menmaatre (Menmaatre-setepenptah), the naming of a king in official documents

FIGURE 16 The lid of a canopic jar of Tuy; from QV80 (Luxor Museum).

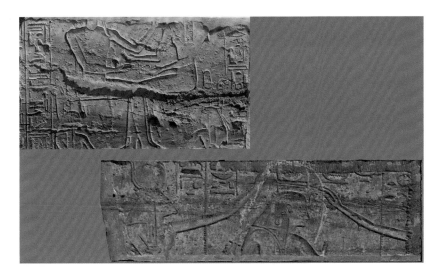

FIGURE 17 Blocks from tableaux, originally from the Ramesseum and reused in Ptolemaic times at Medinet Habu, depicting the conception and birth of Rameses II. Top: Tuy with Amun-Re, fused with Sethy I at the moment of conception; bottom: the upper part of the scene of her giving birth to Rameses II; Medinet Habu, Small Temple.

FIGURE 18 Image of Tuy from the back of the gateway between the Hypostyle Hall and the Second Court at the Ramesseum.

(other than in a dateline) normally implies that they are deceased. Accordingly, Baketwernel's 'Menmaatre' would appear to have been Sethy I, although no trace of her tomb, nor anything else about her, seems to survive outside this papyrus.

There has been considerable debate over whether a woman named Henutmire was a third child of Sethy I or a daughter of Rameses II.[10] However, her representation on the back pillar of a statue of Queen Tuy (fig. 19) would seem more appropriate to Henutmire being Tuy's daughter, rather than a granddaughter.[11] Henutmire certainly went on to marry Rameses II and have a tomb in the Valley of the Queens at Thebes (QV75),[12] of similar plan to the rather larger tombs of Tuy and Henutmire's sister-in-law, Nefertiry (QV66). Decoration was carried out in raised relief, with images of Henutmire and deities, together with tableaux derived from the Book of the Dead. Although a fragment of one of her canopic jars was found there, the trough of Henutmire's stone coffin was later removed from the tomb and ultimately reused for the burial of the eighth-century Theban king Horsieset I at Medinet Habu.[13]

Until the last years of the Eighteenth Dynasty, the royal family (as against the king himself) had been an inconspicuous entity in Egyptian society and politics. Down to the end of the Fourth Dynasty, royal sons had held important state offices, including the vizierate, but from the early Fifth Dynasty, this ceased to be the case.

Henceforth the sons of the king all but disappeared from the monuments, with only a handful known by name from the remaining span of the Old Kingdom and the whole of the Middle Kingdom. A few more are known from the Second Intermediate Period, and during the Eighteenth Dynasty a number of royal sons began to be appointed to senior priestly offices, and occasionally middle-ranking civil posts. However, where such individuals appeared on official monuments it was by virtue of their formal offices, not their blood. Thus, our knowledge of the vast majority of 'ordinary' Eighteenth Dynasty royal princes comes from the private memorials of nobles who had acted as tutors to the boys in question. These include graffiti, left behind on 'study trips' to such places as the granite islands of the First Cataract and, in particular, the tutors' own tomb-chapels, in which they wished to underline their intimate links with the king. Most royal daughters are likewise known from such private sources.

During the last years of the Eighteenth Dynasty, this policy began to change, with Amenhotep III and Akhenaten both featuring their daughters with them on their monuments, the latter extensively. This was not, however, the case with sons, with Thutmose, the eldest son of Amenhotep III, only being shown by virtue of his office as high priest of Ptah.[14] On the other hand, in one case Akhenaten's son, Tutankhaten (later King Tutankhamun), was apparently shown together with one of his sisters (and probably their parents) on a temple wall at Amarna, although only two blocks with the label texts of the prince and princess can currently be identified.[15]

While the lack of known sons of Tutankhamun and Horemheb, and the destroyed or usurped state of the monuments of Ay (whose own son Nakhtmin is known only from a private statue),[16] obscures how this development might have been taken forward during the last years of the Eighteenth Dynasty, the new line of Rameses I had in contrast no qualms concerning the depiction of royal children by virtue of birth alone. Thus, in his temple at Abydos (see pages 31–43), we find Sethy I accompanied by Prince Rameses on four occasions in one particular corridor (fig. 20), the most important being where Rameses is shown with the king, reading a prayer to the royal ancestors, listed in a long chronological sequence (fig. 38). The presence of the crown prince in this context can hardly have been coincidental, and it seems clear that the tableaux in the corridor were together intended to link the commoner-born Sethy and his heir with the line of ancient kings that stretched back to Menes, the founder of the Egyptian monarchy. A similar desire to present the newly minted royal family as wholly fitting into the continuum of pharaonic kingship may well have lain behind Rameses's later large-scale presentation of his numerous family on his monuments.

FIGURE 19 Statue of Tuy, reworked during the reign of Rameses II from one of Tiye, wife of Amenhotep III. On the rear pillar is an image of the King's daughter and the King's wife Henutmire, the lower part of which was erroneously restored in early modern times (Vatican 22678).

FIGURE 20 Sethy I and Crown Prince Rameses in the Gallery of the Lists in the king's Abydos temple (fig. 39).

For many years most scholars believed that prior to the end of Sethy's reign, Prince Rameses had been advanced to the role of coregent or 'prince regent,' endowed with all the trappings of kingship except for his own regnal years.[17] This was based on a number of strands of evidence, in particular the juxtaposition of representations of Sethy I and Rameses II in the Hypostyle Hall at Karnak (for which see page 51) and in Sethy's memorial temple (pages 72–79), plus Rameses's pseudoautobiographical *Inscription Dédicatoire*, inscribed on the façade of his father's temple at Abydos (pages 32–33).[18] The latter includes a summary of Rameses's princely career, including an account of his coronation while his father yet lived. However, the terminology used for the latter makes it quite possible that it describes a prospective wish, seen through the lens of Rameses's undoubted kingship by the time that the *Inscription* was composed. It also has much in common with Hatshepsut's Coronation Inscription at Deir el-Bahari,[19] in which she describes her coronation by her own father, Thutmose I—yet as a point of fact she did not actually become queen until Year 7 of Thutmose III, long after Thutmose I's death.[20]

Looking more closely at juxtapositions of the two kings in temple decoration, long taken as the fruit of 'joint' work in the buildings, it becomes clear that these were actually the outcome of Rameses continuing work begun, but not completed, at his father's death, with the occasional inclusion of a figure of the now-deified Sethy[21] for reasons of filial piety.[22] Other apparent anachronisms that have been cited as indicating that Rameses reigned alongside his father are by no means definitive. For example, the inclusion of Viceroy Amenemopet (who had certainly left office before the end of Sethy's reign) in Rameses II's early battle reliefs in his temple at Beit el-Wali may simply reflect the young king conflating episodes from his career as crown prince into those of his first military operations as king.[23]

Although it seems highly likely that Rameses took part in military operations while crown prince, his fullest-known titles do not actually include anything specifically to do with combat operations.[24]

He was certainly an *imy-r mš' wr*—normally translated as Great Chief of the Army ('Generalissimo')—but with the qualification "for all monuments," implying that his role was managing manpower for royal building projects. This lines up with Rameses's later statement that while yet a prince he had held responsibility for work at Sethy I's Abydos temple.[25]

Thus, there is no persuasive evidence for Rameses having acquired any kind of kingship prior to his father's death. Indeed, in contrast to what was long held as self-evident, it is now becoming increasingly likely that the very concept of coregency as seen during the Middle Kingdom, whereby the heir to the throne was made full co-ruler with his father,[26] was not actually employed during the New Kingdom.[27] Of the various potential coregencies proposed over the years,[28] the only ones where the evidence seems wholly unequivocal (that is, where the co-rulers are actually shown interacting together) are two where a woman held the co-rulership in question.[29] In all other cases, the evidence may either be a likely ancient scribal error or wholly circumstantial and/or capable of alternative interpretation.[30] The case of the alleged association between Sethy I and Rameses II very much falls into this second category.

The Restorer King

The desire just discussed to cement the legitimacy of his line may have prompted Sethy I to engage enthusiastically in the restoration of monuments mutilated during the persecution of the god Amun under Akhenaten.[31] During this episode (see pages 5–6), both two- and three-dimensional images of the god, as well as his names and titles, had been mutilated, with some attention paid to his wife, Mut, as well; other gods were largely left alone, except in cases of seeming 'collateral damage.'

Restoration of such damage had begun under Tutankhamun, with reliefs re-carved as necessary and many divine statues created with the young king's features. The amount of work required in restoring reliefs varied with the amount of damage originally done: in some cases it was possible to smooth down the area once occupied by Amun's names and texts and simply re-carve them; in others, a whole tableau might be cut back and the whole thing re-carved, as far as possible reproducing the original subject matter. Restorations under Tutankhamun (and later by Ay and Horemheb) were sometimes accompanied by the addition of a short text recording the act, but not in any kind of standardized way.

However, things became far more systematized under Sethy I,[32] who not only continued the process of restoring material that still remained in a damaged state but also 're-restored' material already dealt with by Tutankhamun (and probably Ay as well).[33] Behind this repetition of effort presumably lay the fact that, while ultimately an 'orthodox' king, Tutankhamun had been tainted by his ancestry, with his monuments usurped by his successors: his restorations were thus presumably felt to be blemished by association, in particular as the faces of re-carved human-headed deities bore the visage of either the discredited king or of his queen.

Sethy's restorations are characterized by the use of a standard set of accompanying formulae naming the king himself, with the name of the originator of the monument usually retained in the final version of the tableau or text in question (fig. 21). There were, however, cases where Sethy appropriated at least part of the main texts of a piece, one example being the obelisks of Hatshepsut at Karnak. Here, Sethy's names replaced some examples of those of the piece's authoress, perhaps in an attempt to create a link with not only her but also Thutmose I and III, who were also named on the obelisks. Another case in point is in the extensive work done on Karnak's Pylon VIII, where the decoration now included Sethy receiving votes of thanks for his efforts from Amun himself.

Monuments restored by Sethy I are found throughout Egypt, and in some cases not only were a structure's images and texts restored but the monument itself was extended as well, one likely example being at the rock-cut Speos Artemidos (Istabl Antar), near Beni Hasan (fig. 22), where the inner shrine was decorated, and probably cut, by Sethy I. In the pronaos, decorated by Hatshepsut, figures of the female king mutilated under Thutmose III were reworked as representations of Sethy, while additional scenes seem to have been Sethy originals (fig. 23). A great text commemorating the king's work at the temple is dated to Year 1, while one suspects that much of the restoration program

FIGURE 21 Lintel of Amenhotep II from Bubastis, entirely recut when restored by Sethy I; his restoration text now occupies the center column of the composition (BM EA1103).

FIGURE 22 The Speos Artemidos (Istabl Antar), at Batn el-Baqara, near Beni Hasan, dedicated to Pakhet, originally constructed by Hatshepsut but extensively restored by Sethy I.

FIGURE 23 Scene from the entrance to the sanctuary of the Speos Artemidos, showing Sethy I offering to Pakhet.

across Egypt was undertaken during the earliest years of the reign.

Naturally, the largest concentration of restorations were at Thebes, Amun's principal cult center, with some thirty areas of Karnak temple today exhibiting examples of Sethy's rework. Some twenty surviving cases exist at Luxor temple, where Sethy also resumed and completed the decoration of the southernmost part of the Colonnade Hall, left unfinished by Tutankhamun. On the West Bank, a number of pieces exhibiting Sethy I restorations survive, but the scale of the later destruction of structures there obscures the likely scale of work carried out.

At Tod, the bark station was restored by Sethy, but there are no signs there of divine figures having been damaged by Akhenaten, so this work may have been a general refurbishment unrelated to any prior iconoclastic vandalism. Further south, at El-Kab, mutilated figures of Amun and the goddess Nekhbet were renewed in the desert temple of Amenhotep III, as was the case with images of Amun in various structures on Elephantine island at Aswan and in the Nubian temple of Amada. Also in Nubia, the temple built at Sesebi in honor of the Aten was taken over and redecorated for Amun by Sethy.

A still-open question concerning the aftermath of the Amarna episode is how the cult of the Aten—as against the memory of its patron—was regarded by the forces of the counterreformation. Indeed, it has been suggested that a Memphite sanctuary of the Aten was still operational under Sethy I, since a papyrus,[34] probably from Memphis and generally dated to that king's reign, records a shipment of a batch of wood from a "Mansion of the Aten."[35] On the other hand, the provenance, date, and significance of the papyrus have been questioned, with the suggestion that the papyrus actually refers to a shipment of lumber from the dismantlement of a sanctuary at Amarna. Nevertheless, it remains possible that at least one Aten sanctuary was indeed still operating under Sethy I,[36] and thus that it may have been several decades after Akhenaten's death before his god had been fully absorbed back into Re-Horakhty, of whom the Aten had originally been an aspect. In this connection, it is worth noting that the Nubian site of Kawa (with its Amun temple!) was still called *Gm-'Itn* many centuries later, in Napatan times.

The Builder King

From the Delta to the Memphite Region

Although his reign lasted only a decade, Sethy I was responsible for initiating a large number of building projects throughout Egypt, although many were unfinished at his death and only finally completed by his successors. The dynasty's Delta origins are probably reflected by the king's erection of a palace complex at Qantir, a northeastern site that lay adjacent to the ancient Tell el-Daba, capital of the Palestinian Hyksos kings of the Second Intermediate Period. During the reign of Rameses II, Qantir would grow into a vast metropolis that, under the name of *Pr-R'mssw*, would become the effective capital of Egypt until the end of the New Kingdom.

Lying on the now-vanished Pelusiac branch of the Nile, Qantir held an important strategic location, both from the point of view of seaborne trade from the Levant and further afield, and as a gateway for military campaigns northward into Syria-Palestine (for which see pages 58–66). However, the silting up of its Nile branch during the Twentieth Dynasty removed the city's economic basis, and over the next few centuries its buildings were dismantled to reuse their stone, much being used at the new northeastern capital, Tanis (San el-Hagar), some twenty kilometers to the north. Accordingly, only the traces of building foundations survive under today's fields, together with a few architectural fragments, including a memorial made by Sethy I for his father, Rameses I.[37] Faience inlays also survive from a door of the palace of Sethy, as do the remains of an associated military/industrial complex, which included metalworking facilities and a hall associated with the fitting out of chariots. Heliopolis, at the apex of the Delta and since the earliest times the center of the cult of the sun god Re, has, like Qantir, been extensively denuded by stone robbery in ancient and modern times and is also now largely covered by suburbs of Cairo. Only one fragment naming Sethy I has thus far been found at Heliopolis, although the lower part of a contemporary model of the new frontage added to the main temple under the king was found nearby, with sockets for a pylon and abutting walls as

FIGURE 24 Base of a model of the new pylon and outer courtyard added to the temple of Re at Heliopolis by Sethy I (Brooklyn 49.183).

well as for the obelisks and statues that would flank the approach ramp (fig. 24). However, various other items bearing the king's name are shown by their texts to derive from these and other structures erected by Sethy I at Heliopolis.[38]

Of obelisks raised by Sethy I at Heliopolis, one complete example survives, along with the fragments of others. All had been removed from Heliopolis in Hellenistic and Roman times: the complete one, unfinished at Sethy's death and actually erected by Rameses II (fig. 25) was later (in 30 BC) transported to Rome (see pages 119–20). Two now-incomplete examples had been moved at some point to Alexandria and eventually became submerged in the harbor there (fig. 26). One of these was made of quartzite, rather than the more usual granite, and was of relatively modest size; two similar obelisks were abandoned unfinished in the Gebel Gulab quarry at Aswan (fig. 27).

At Memphis, a single foundation deposit survives from a former temple of Sethy I, while a small chapel dedicated to Ptah remains standing within the Memphite ruin field, where various blocks have also been found.[39] In the adjacent necropolis of Saqqara, a burial of an Apis bull, in Serapeum Isolated Tomb F, has been dated to Sethy's reign by a fragment from its chapel.[40] The tomb comprised a main chamber, with a subsidiary room that housed fourteen pottery jars containing ashes and burnt bones, apparently from a ritual in which the dead bull was partly burnt. Only four largely undamaged canopic lids survived from the interment itself. Two private tombs at Saqqara are known to have belonged to individuals who lived under Sethy I (fig. 65).[41]

FIGURE 25 Obelisk begun by Sethy I and completed by Rameses II, originally erected at Heliopolis, and now in the Piazza del Popolo in Rome (see pages 120–21 and fig. 113).

FIGURE 26 Section of granite obelisk of Sethy I, showing the king as a Seth-headed sphinx before Re-Atum; originally from Heliopolis, found in the harbor at Alexandria (Kom el-Dikka, Alexandria).

FIGURE 27 Upper part of an unfinished quartzite obelisk of Sethy I, found in the quarry of Gebel Gulab at Aswan.

Abydos

Among the most impressive of all surviving monuments of Sethy I is the temple[42] and adjacent cenotaph[43] that he constructed at Abydos, holy city of Osiris (fig. 28). As with most of his other structures, the temple was not completed during Sethy I's lifetime, with the outer courts and pylons entirely decorated (if not built) by Rameses II and significant parts of the temple proper also decorated by the younger king. The cenotaph would not be finished until even later—under Merenptah, who came to the throne some seven decades after Sethy I's death.

The site chosen for the complex was in the southern part of the main necropolis area at Abydos, within the Old/Middle Kingdom South Cemetery, around a kilometer south of the main Osiris temple at Kom el-Sultan. It was also one and a half kilometers east of the Early Dynastic royal necropolis at Umm el-Qaab, regarded since the Middle Kingdom as also the physical burial place of Osiris.[44] As such, Sethy's complex lay at an important nexus of the ancient cult centers of the site; it also lay three kilometers north of the pyramid complex of Ahmose I, founder of the New Kingdom, with whom Sethy's father, Rameses I, had implicitly linked himself through his prenomen (page 18).

The site also lay directly south of the chapel that Sethy built for Rameses I, as already noted (pages 12–13).[45] Surrounded by a brick enclosure wall, the chapel was entered by an inscribed limestone gateway giving access to an open courtyard, which sloped up to the sanctuary. Of classic form, with a cavetto cornice and torus molding, externally it was just over four meters wide and six meters deep, its façade decorated with figures of Sethy, accompanied by texts dedicating the structure to his father. The decoration of the interior focused on the cult of the dead king and the memorialization of his family. It would seem likely that this structure was one of the earliest works of Sethy's reign, and preceded the foundation of the king's Abydene temple.

The basic layout of that temple followed that of most New Kingdom examples, with a series of terraced courtyards, fronted by ramps and pylons, leading up to the façade of the inner part of the structure (fig. 29). These outer sections of Sethy's temple were decorated under Rameses II, but it remains unclear how far their construction might have progressed under Sethy I. Rameses was also responsible for decorating the portico at the rear of the Second Court (B) that gave access to the First Hypostyle Hall of the temple (C), although its actual construction seems to have been undertaken under Sethy (unlike the portico at the back of the First Courtyard [A], which was certainly erected by Rameses).

The design of the main temple's portico was altered by Rameses, who blocked up all but the centermost of the seven doors with which Sethy's original design had pierced it. Each of these had been aligned with one of the seven cult sanctuaries that formed

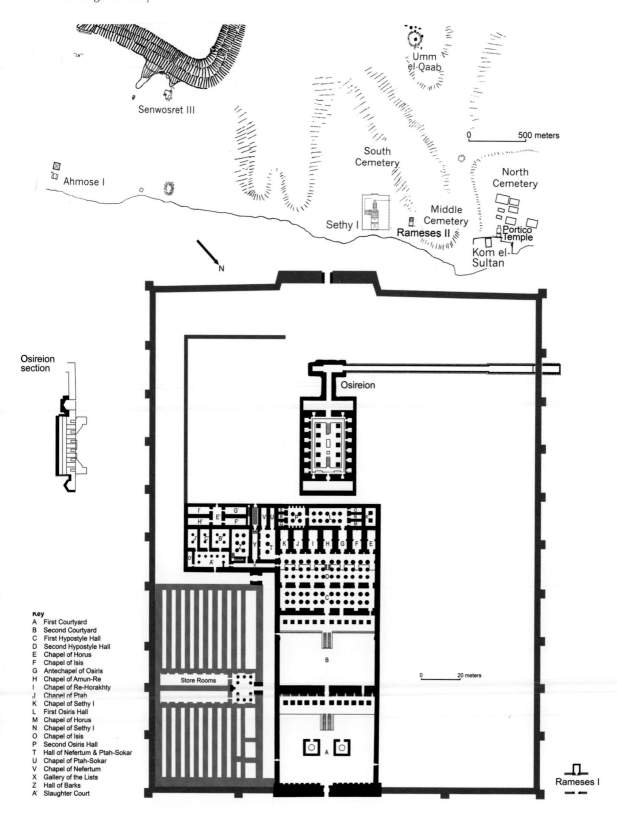

Senwosret III

Umm
el-Qaab

0   500 meters

Ahmose I

South
Cemetery

North
Cemetery

Sethy I

Middle
Cemetery

Rameses II

Portico
Temple

Kom el-
Sultan

N

Osireion
section

Osireion

Store Rooms

0   20 meters

Rameses I

Key
A First Courtyard
B Second Courtyard
C First Hypostyle Hall
D Second Hypostyle Hall
E Chapel of Horus
F Chapel of Isis
G Antechapel of Osiris
H Chapel of Amun-Re
I Chapel of Re-Horakhty
J Chapel of Ptah
K Chapel of Sethy I
L First Osiris Hall
M Chapel of Horus
N Chapel of Sethy I
O Chapel of Isis
P Second Osiris Hall
T Hall of Nefertum & Ptah-Sokar
U Chapel of Ptah-Sokar
V Chapel of Nefertum
X Gallery of the Lists
Z Hall of Barks
A' Slaughter Court

FIGURE 28 The complex of Sethy I at Abydos, with a map of the Abydos site.

a distinctive feature of the temple (see further below). The broad surface created by this blocking was used to inscribe Rameses II's *Inscription Dédicatoire*, which includes this account of the completion of his father's monuments:[46]

FIGURE 29 Façade of the main part of the temple of Sethy I at Abydos.

> Now, the Temple of Menmaatre, its front and rear were (still) under construction when he entered heaven. There were none who completed its monuments, none who erected its pillars upon its terrace; its statue (lay) upon the ground . . . , its sacred offerings had ceased to function, and the temple staff likewise.
>
> Then His Person said to the chancellor who was beside him: "Speak and summon the courtiers, the royal notables, all the generals, the overseers of works—as many of them as there are—and the chiefs of secrets." Thereupon they were brought before His Person . . . . Then His Person said to them: "See I have summoned you concerning a matter that is before me: . . . See, his temple was under my supervision . . . I will make it great in renewing its monuments . . . . I will build up the walls of the temple of the one who begot me. I shall put in charge a man of my choice to direct this work in it. I shall make good that which is missing from its walls, [I shall complete] its pylon-towers . . . , I shall roof his house, I shall erect his pillars, I shall set stones in the foundation-trenches."[47]

One rather doubts that the temple had truly been abandoned by its builders and functionaries on Sethy I's death, with the royal authority of Rameses needed to get work restarted. Instead, it is probable that the text conforms to a typical genre of Egyptian laudatory literature, where a situation is described as particularly dire to emphasize the piety, wisdom, and energy of the protagonist in resolving it. Nevertheless, as already noted, it was indeed Rameses II who undertook a significant part of the construction and decoration of the temple.

While most of the monument was built of limestone, the two hypostyle halls also featured columns of sandstone. In the First Hypostyle Hall (fig. 30), although it had been fully decorated in raised relief by Sethy I, all images were later converted into sunk relief by Rameses II in his own name. In contrast, the Second Hypostyle Hall (D, figs. 31, 125) and the inner parts of the temple retained its original adornment, comprising exquisite raised relief of a quality rarely paralleled in Egyptian art. The scenes here and throughout the temple comprised almost entirely images of the gods and the king interacting with them (fig. 32). The reliefs on the west wall of the hall, along with some on the north wall, had been both carved and painted by Sethy's death, but the rest had only been carved, and in

FIGURE 30 The First Hypostyle Hall at Abydos.

some cases still awaited some of their final detailing, when work was abandoned.

FIGURE 31 The Second Hypostyle Hall.

At the back of the hall opened the seven aforementioned cult chapels, one of the most unusual features of the temple: most Egyptian temples were dedicated to one deity, or at most a triad. As noted previously, each originally was to have its own processional route from the main portico, but these were blocked off by Rameses II; both hypostyle halls, however, retained openings in their rear walls. The central chapel (H) was dedicated to Amun-Re, with the flanking ones on the north belonging to the Abydene triad of Osiris (G), Isis (F), and Horus (E), and on the south to Re-Horakhty (I), Ptah (J), and Sethy I himself (K). All were of the same basic barrel-roofed, two-roomed form (fig. 33), except for that of Osiris, which was actually the antechapel to a pair of pillared halls and subsidiary chapels (L–S, figs. 34–36). All these elements of the temple had been carved by Sethy's death, with the Amun chapel and much of the Osiris suite painted as well.

FIGURE 32 Niche in the Second Hypostyle Hall, showing the king offering to Mut; Sethy's stooping pose before the deity is distinctive of the temple iconography of the reign.

FIGURE 33 The chapel of Ptah, fully carved but left unpainted.

FIGURE 34 The outer room of the Osiris suite, looking toward the inner rooms.

FIGURE 35 The main hall of the Osiris suite, with the shrine of Sethy I visible at the end.

South of these sanctuaries was an extension to the temple that gave the whole building an unusual L-shaped plan: most Egyptian temples were essentially symmetrical around their main axis. Part of the extension was occupied by a complex dedicated to the Memphite gods Ptah-Sokar and Nefertum (T, fig. 37), the rest by a complex of rooms and corridors, most approached from the Second Hypostyle Hall via the Gallery of the Lists (X, fig. 39). The east wall of this had the king and Prince Rameses making offerings to various deities (fig. 20), but most of the opposite wall was taken up with a scene in which the king accompanies Rameses, who reads a prayer to the former kings of Egypt (fig. 38). This whole tableau seems likely intended to cement the arriviste new dynasty into the narrative of Egyptian history, stretching back to the Unification (cf. page 18).

The composition of this list of dedicants is interesting both from the point of view of which kings were included and also those who were left out. Little surprise is occasioned by the omission of the kings from Akhenaten through Ay, while Hatshepsut's absence could be explained either by her posthumous disgrace or by the fact she only ever ruled as a coregent. However, while a long sequence of rulers of the Memphite line of the early First Intermediate Period was provided, those of the whole Second Intermediate Period were omitted. This is difficult to explain in principled terms, and perhaps the most likely solution is simply that the artist had a finite space to fill and that an 'all or nothing' approach was taken when faced

FIGURE 36 The Horus shrine of the Osiris suite.

with nearly one hundred names attributable to the Thirteenth through Seventeenth Dynasties. On the other hand, the names available for the Seventh/Eighth Dynasties were a more manageable proposition and probably conveniently made up the number of cartouches required to fill the available space.[48]

The Gallery gave access to the Hall of the Barks (Z, fig. 40), decorated by Rameses II, and also to the Slaughter Court (A', fig. 41) and its subsidiary rooms (B',

FIGURE 37 The Hall of Nefertum and Ptah-Sokar, looking west.

FIGURE 38 The so-called king list in the Abydos temple in the Gallery of the Lists,
with Prince Rameses reading a prayer to ancient rulers named on the rest of the wall.

FIGURE 39 The Gallery of the Lists.

FIGURE 40 The Hall of Barks.

FIGURE 41 The Slaughter Court.

FIGURE 42 The Osireion from the southwest, showing the entrance hall on the left.

D', and J'), where sacrificial animals were dealt with. It also led to a corridor (Y), decorated under Rameses II, with a stairway to a vast courtyard at the rear of the temple, which could also be accessed via a brick pylon facing west, toward the Umm el-Qaab cemetery and its tomb of Osiris.

It was in this courtyard that Sethy I founded a structure without a precise parallel among Egyptian monuments. This was the so-called Osireion, a stone-built structure sunk in the ground and originally topped with a tumulus (fig. 42). Named "Menmaatre in an Effective Spirt for Osiris," its exact purpose remains obscure, but its decoration with material appropriate to a tomb indicates that it was some form of cenotaph. Its construction began with that of a limestone retaining wall, against which its innermost chamber was constructed (again in limestone). Work then continued westward in sandstone and granite. If the sandstone was part of a large order placed with the Gebel el-Silsila quarries in Year 6 (see page 54), this would place the second phase of the Osireion during the final third of Sethy I's reign, explaining why the inner chamber was the only part of the monument whose decoration had been completed prior to the king's death.

The Osireion's interior was accessed via a shaft just outside the northern enclosure wall of the entire Sethy complex, at its western end. From here, a brick-vaulted passage ran southward for thirty-two meters, after which it became faced with sandstone. The extant decoration of the corridor was the work of Sethy I's grandson Merenptah, although it appears that the carving was done on the basis of original cartoons dating to Sethy's reign. It comprised figures of the king and extracts from the Book of Gates (west wall: on this composition, and others employed in the Osireion, see pages 81–84), and lists of

FIGURE 43 The main hall of the Osireion, showing the 'island' surrounded by water, and the cuttings that were apparently intended for a symbolic sarcophagus and canopic chest. In the background can be seen the break in the hills beyond Umm el-Qaab, possibly envisaged as a gateway to the Beyond.

denizens of the underworld (east). Merenptah was also responsible for the carving of the decoration (comprising elements from the Book of the Dead) of the antechamber that opened out of the passageway sixty meters further on.

From here, a sloping passageway, also decorated with more extracts from the Book of the Dead, led into a large transverse room, its roof preserving traces of swimming figures and an image of Nut—all again carved under Merenptah. Beyond lay the Great Hall, its roof supported by granite pillars whose resemblance to those of the Old Kingdom Valley Building of Khaefre at Giza led early scholars to suggest that it was actually an ancient structure remodeled by Sethy I. However, the main structure of the Osireion is composed of limestone and sandstone, while cramps holding granite blocks together bore the names of Sethy, making even a rebuilding of an ancient structure all but impossible.

Its east wall was decorated by Merenptah in poor sunk relief but was otherwise devoid of decoration. The central part of the hall was surrounded by a channel, intended to be filled by subsoil water so as to take the form of an island, on which cavities which may have held a symbolic sarcophagus and a canopic chest were cut (fig. 43). The whole hall was surrounded by small annexes, a doorway in the back of the one opposite the entrance giving access to a final transverse chamber made of limestone, unlike the rest of the Osireion. It is possible that this was intended to have been isolated from the rest of the cenotaph, the access passage being for use during construction only. It was the only part of the building actually decorated under Sethy I himself, including an enigmatic 'dramatic' religious text on the west wall, together with an astronomical ceiling.

Apart from his temple and cenotaph, and the chapel he built for Rameses I, evidence of other activities of Sethy I at Abydos is restricted to a few artistic and architectural fragments (fig. 44).[49] Bricks naming Sethy from the foundation platform of the 'Portal Temple' (fig. 45), largely built and decorated by Rameses II, indicate that Sethy founded the structure, while he may also have made contributions to the main Osiris temple at Kom el-Sultan, directly to the east.

FIGURE 44 The more complete of three similar statues of Sethy I kneeling to present offerings (the others are now in Dallas and Sorrento, Italy); the surviving texts indicate that they were originally dedicated at Abydos (MMA 22.2.21).

FIGURE 45 The Portal Temple at Abydos, begun by Sethy I although completed and decorated by Rameses II.

The high priesthood of the latter temple was held during the reign of Sethy I successively by To-Tjay, Hat, and then Mery, whose son Wenennefer would take the office under Rameses II. A number of those who worked for Sethy's great Abydos foundation are also known, although at much more junior levels.[50]

Thebes East

FIGURE 46 Map of Thebes.

It is the Theban area (fig. 46) that contains the largest volume of surviving material from Sethy I's reign. On the East Bank, we

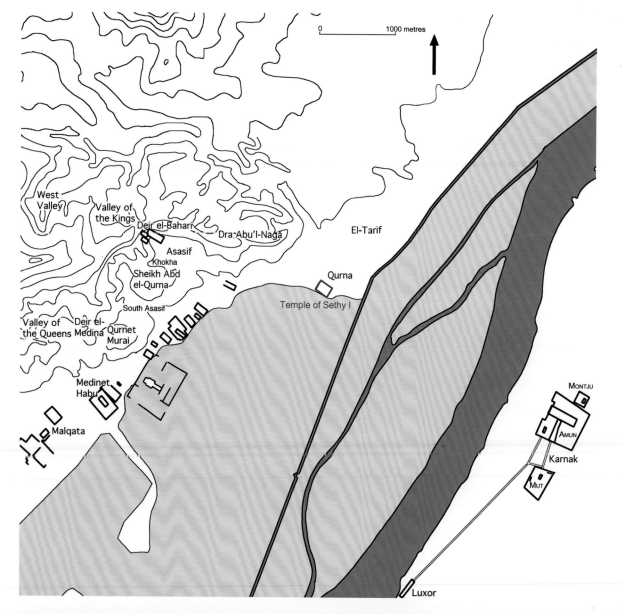

have already noted Sethy I's work in completing the decoration of the Luxor temple, and his acts of restoration at Karnak, but it was his constructional activities at the latter that represented the king's greatest contribution to the temples in this area (fig. 47). At the beginning of the Amarna Period, the western façade of the temple of Amun-Re had comprised what is now Pylon III, built by Amenhotep III, and its porch, decorated during the first years of Akhenaten (while yet Amenhotep IV). Some three decades later, the temple was extended sixty meters further west by Horemheb's construction of Pylon II on land only relatively recently left dry by the ongoing westward retreat of the Nile.[51]

FIGURE 47 Aerial view of the temple of Amun-Re at Karnak, showing the main west-east axis, from the Thirtieth Dynasty Pylon I (top) to the Festival Hall of Thutmose III (bottom right), and Pylons VIII and VII on the southern axis, to the left.

Whether the space thus created was intended as an open courtyard or as a peristyle or hypostyle space has been much discussed, but no firm evidence exists that anything was actually done under Horemheb, beyond the construction of the pylon. Past arguments in favor of his having done so have been essentially based on the presence of reliefs of Rameses I on the rear of the pylon (fig. 48), which clearly formed part of the decoration of the eventual Great Hypostyle Hall.[52] If indeed carved under Rameses, the brevity of his reign would mean that the hall must have been well underway before the death of

Horemheb. However, the reliefs in question are in fact integral in both layout and style with those executed under Sethy I—and contrast in style with some of Rameses I in the entrance to Pylon II, which seem to be certainly contemporary with Rameses's reign.

Accordingly, it seems clear that it was Sethy I who transformed a space left essentially empty by Horemheb into the stupendous Great Hypostyle Hall, its roof supported by a forest of 146 columns, of which twelve taller, heavier examples facilitated an axial clerestory roof (figs. 49, 50). The whole hall seems to have been structurally complete by the end of Sethy I's reign: its columns, plus the north and south walls joining together Pylons II and III. These walls were each pierced by a gateway, which bracketed a north-south processional way across the Hall.

However, as with so many of Sethy's monuments, only part of the Hall had actually been decorated by his death. The structure had been built by filling it with sand as the walls and columns rose, and then dressing and decorating their surfaces as they were revealed by the removal of the

FIGURE 48 Rameses I, as shown in the top register of the decoration of the rear of Pylon II—some of the very earliest adornment of the Hypostyle Hall. The images of Rameses alternate with those of Sethy I, and clearly represent Sethy's commemoration of his father.

FIGURE 49 The Hypostyle Hall at Karnak from the northeast; to the left is Pylon III,
built by Amenhotep III, and in the foreground the colonnade of Shabaka.

FIGURE 50 The vast scale of the Hypostyle Hall is demonstrated here; to the left is the back of Pylon II.

soil. This process had begun once the uppermost courses, architraves, and roofing had been put in place. Thus, the first parts of the Hall to be decorated were the architraves and abaci of the columns of the central clerestory. Next came the interior and exterior of the northern gateway: on the outside were carved sunk-relief figures of the king smiting enemies (fig. 60); inside, the figures were in raised relief, showing the king before Amun and other members of the Theban triad.

The latter images were, however, soon reworked to show the king in all cases bowing toward the deities (fig. 51), rather than standing erect before them as in some cases. This humble pose of the king vis-à-vis the gods is distinctive of temple representations of Sethy I and, where they were later usurped by Rameses II or other kings, they were usually changed to the more usual upright royal stance. The rest of the interior of the north wall was then decorated with a wide range of ritual scenes incorporating the motif of the bowing king, but even then some elements were subject to adjustment, seemingly while the artists refined their style.

Artistic stability had apparently been reached by the time that work on the north wall was complete, and attention shifted to the

FIGURE 51 Part of Sethy I's decoration of the north interior wall of Karnak's Hypostyle Hall. The king's figure shows a number of reworkings, the earlier phases of which would have been concealed by plaster and paint.

east and west walls. These had been essentially completed and effort had started to be applied to the southern half of the Hall, including a number of complete tableaux on the west wall, when Sethy died. The 'regular' columns in the northern half of the Hall had also by then been decorated (generally with a single tableau facing the axis/axes of the Hall), but the southern ones, and the remaining interior wall surfaces of the Hall, had at most been laid out in colored cartoons only. The shafts of the 'big' columns supporting the clerestory seem never to have received any adornment under Sethy.

Rameses II completed his father's work in sunk relief, and also usurped and re-carved Sethy's decoration of the clerestory, as well as some of the architraves spanning the 'regular' columns. Rameses also added reliefs to many of the column surfaces that Sethy had left plain, with the remaining spare spaces later filled in with texts by Rameses IV and Herihor, during the Twentieth and Twenty-first Dynasties. Some of this latter incised work obscured elements of Sethy's original decoration, carried out in extremely fine raised relief, projecting only a few millimeters above the surface.

As far as the exterior walls of the Hall were concerned, the northern wall was adorned with scenes in sunk relief depicting Sethy's military activities (see pages 58–66). The southern exterior wall shows no signs of any planned decoration under Sethy I and was eventually used by Rameses II for a depiction of his Battle of Qadesh. This was later erased and replaced by a sequence belonging to other campaigns in Syria.

Sethy I's building efforts at Karnak seem to have been largely concentrated on the Hypostyle Hall. On the other hand, a pair of bases for colossal statues (later usurped by Rameses III and IV) in front of the southern gateway of the

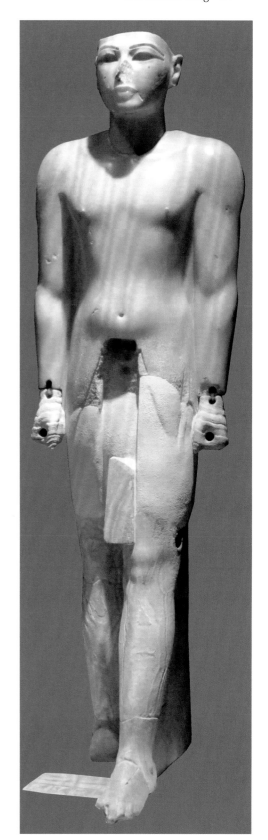

FIGURE 52 A composite statue of Sethy I, made of six pieces of calcite; the missing sections would have been made of other materials. It may have served as the focus of a cult of the king somewhere in the Karnak complex but was found in the great Ptolemaic "Cachette" in the courtyard behind Pylon VII (Luxor Museum ex-Cairo CG42139=JE36692).

FIGURE 53 Granodiorite statue of Amun, Mut, and Sethy I, reassembled from fragments found outside the Festival Hall at Karnak (Cairo CG927 + CG39210 + Karnak-Caracol 543 + Louvre E.11100).

Montju complex suggest that Sethy may have built the original version of the gate (the surviving remains of which date to the Thirtieth Dynasty king Nakhtnebef). Various stelae and pieces of sculpture have been found within the Karnak complex, although their exact original locations generally remain obscure, having been moved and/or reused during later centuries (figs. 52, 53).[53]

No contemporary material survives from any holder of the high priesthood of Amun during the reign of Sethy I, but it is known that the father of the vizier Paser had been high priest, presumably during at least part of Sethy's reign. It has also been suggested that Wepwawetmose might have served during Sethy I's time, but he has also been placed back into the reign of Horemheb.[54]

Thebes West

Across the river from Karnak, Sethy I's own West Theban funerary structures will be the subject of the next chapter. However, a number of monuments and other material dating to his reign have come to light around the Theban necropolis.[55] The king certainly founded a structure at the location later chosen by Rameses II for his own memorial temple, the Ramesseum. Only the foundation trenches and Sethy's foundation deposits survive, the structure having been replaced by one of larger size during the building of the Ramesseum. Its dedication thus remains obscure, although it has been suggested that the later building was a mortuary chapel for Queen Tuy and Rameses II's wife, Nefertiry.

A significant number of items dating to Sethy's reign have come from the royal tomb workers' village of Deir el-Medina, including a doorjamb that may derive from a chapel. The massive expansion of the sculpted area of a king's tomb under Sethy I (see page 84) will have required a significant expansion of the Deir el-Medina workforce, as well as a change in the skill mix of its inhabitants. Among the latter under Sethy I was the workman Sennedjem, whose superbly decorated and intact tomb (TT1) was found in 1886.[56] The chief workmen during the reign included Baki (TT298) and Pashedu (TT3), who continued in office under Rameses II, with Amenemopet (TT215) as scribe of the tomb, the head of administration.

The Eastern Desert

Northeast of Thebes, the presence of three rock stelae in the name of Sethy I in the Wadi Hammamat suggests that graywacke was extracted from the quarries there for his building programs. Also out in the Eastern Desert, but further south, a small settlement was founded in Year 9 at Kanais in the Wadi Abad to support mining operations in the region, being carried out to provide gold for the king's Abydene temple.[57] The village included a temple (figs. 54, 55) whose dedication inscription recorded two visits to the site by the king, the first of which resulted in the establishment of the settlement, and a second during which he dedicated the temple.

FIGURE 54 The site of Kanais; in addition to the rock-cut temple itself, the rock face to the left hosted a number of contemporary stelae.

FIGURE 55 The inner part of the Kanais temple, showing the main sanctuary, with images of the king, Horus of Edfu, and Amun.

It comprised a six-pillared stone-built outer hall, and a four-pillared rock-cut inner hall, with three sanctuaries, each with three deity figures, the central one on all occasions that of the king himself. The remaining deities were the other six who were present in Sethy's temple at Abydos, showing the close link between the two monuments. The preeminence of the king's own cult reflected a general tend beyond the bounds of Egypt proper and is particularly common in Nubian temples.

Gebel el-Silsila

The quarries of Gebel el-Silsila, which lay directly adjacent to the Nile on both sides of the river, were the source for the sandstone employed in building most of the temples of Upper Egypt; those of Sethy I were no exception.[58] A stela of Sethy's Year 6 at Silsila East (now destroyed) recorded the inception of an expedition to quarry material for "monuments for his father Amun-Re, (and for) Osiris, together with his Ennead," probably implying both Theban and Abydene works.

On the riverbank on the opposite side of the river, Sethy created the first of what would be a series of four shrines dedicated to the personification of the Inundation of the Nile (Hapi). A pair of

FIGURE 56 The Royal Shrines at Silsila West, dedicated to the Inundation, constructed by Sethy I (on the left and largely destroyed), Rameses II, and Merenptah.

columns supported a portico sheltering a stela; unfortunately, much of the shrine has now collapsed into the river, destroying, among other things, the record of the date of its construction (fig. 56). A little way upstream, at Kom Ombo, a stela indicates that work was carried out there by Sethy at the joint temple of Sobek and Haroeris. [59]

Aswan

While nothing survives of Sethy I on Elephantine island, the ancient core of Aswan, fragments from a building or buildings associated with the local gods exist.[60] Rock inscriptions also date to his time, two from Year 9 recording the quarrying of a number of colossal statues and obelisks. These seem to have been finished and inscribed after Sethy I's death by Rameses II, the colossi and two of the obelisks ultimately adorning the façade and forecourtyard that Rameses added to Luxor temple. At least one other obelisk had been partially inscribed at Sethy's death and, with Rameses's names added alongside those of his father, was erected at Heliopolis (see page 29). As noted above, two unfinished obelisks of Sethy I were left behind in the Gebel Gulab quartzite quarry at Aswan.

Nubia

Early in the New Kingdom, Egyptian control of Nubia had been extended to a point around the Abu Hamid Reach, between the Fourth and Fifth Cataracts: inscriptions of Thutmose I and III at Kurgus seem to mark the formal boundary.[61] From the beginning

FIGURE 57 Sethy I's Qasr Ibrim rock stela, with the king slaying an enemy at the top; the viceroy Amenemopet is depicted at the bottom-left; now displayed at New Kalabsha.

of the Eighteenth Dynasty, Egypt's Nubian possessions had been organized as a viceroyalty, with Amenemopet, son of Paser, already viceroy under Ay and Horemheb, fulfilling the role for most of Sethy I's reign (fig. 57). Toward the very end of the reign he was succeeded by Iuny, who continued in office under Rameses II.

Unlike Rameses II, who would create many temples in Nubia, Sethy's activities there seem to have been limited.[62] He seems to have founded the fortified town of Aksha (Serra West), on the Second Cataract, late in his reign, although most of the decoration of the temple there was undertaken by Rameses II. Another foundation was Amara West, at that time an island in the Nile, just upstream of the Dal Cataract.[63] A little over one hundred meters square, it had a fortified enclosure wall, a quarter of its area being occupied by a temple, completed and decorated by Rameses II.

Sethy may also have undertaken work in the old Middle Kingdom fortress at Quban, with some blocks possibly later removed across the river to Dakka for reuse. A kiosk was constructed at Amada, southwest of the Thutmoside temple, and a hypostyle hall was added to the Amun temple at Gebel Barkal (fig. 58), the religious capital of Upper Nubia. From the latter came a fragmentary stela, dated to

FIGURE 58 The temple of Amun at Gebel Barkal, with hall B503, constructed under Sethy I. The temple seems to have been begun under Akhenaten, presumably as a sun sanctuary, but subsequently rebuilt and extended.

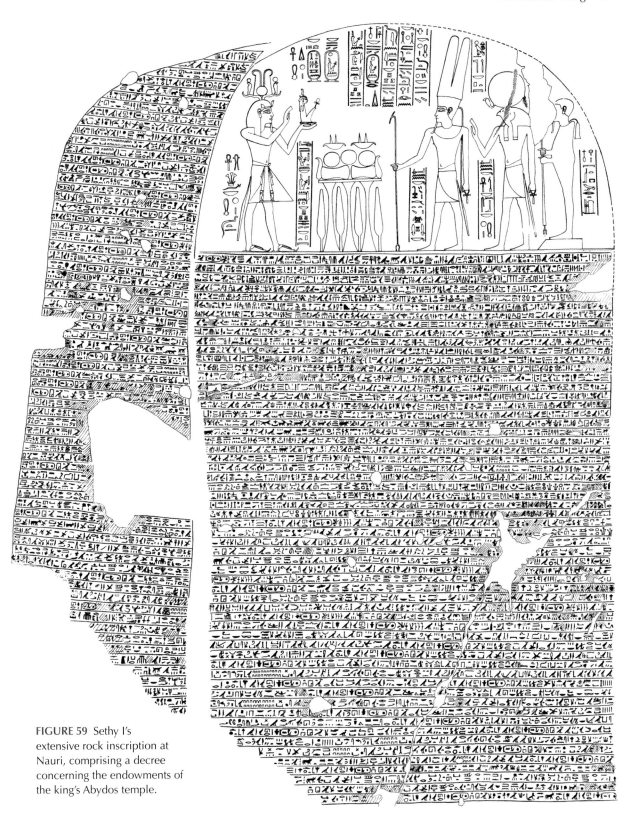

FIGURE 59 Sethy I's extensive rock inscription at Nauri, comprising a decree concerning the endowments of the king's Abydos temple.

IV *šmw* 12/13 in Year 9[64]—the latest date known from the reign of Sethy I (see further page 69).

Various stelae were also erected or inscribed into rock surfaces in other parts of Nubia. One of them, at Nauri, dated to Year 4, dealt with the management of estates established to provide an endowment for the Abydos temple (fig. 59), while others seem to be more local acts of royal commemoration. In the Nubian Western Desert, a stela was erected during Year 4 at the Kurkur Oasis.[65] This marked the western boundary of Egyptian control in the west, the stela recording a formal act of designation.

The Warrior King

As already noted (pages 50, 51), the northern exterior walls of the Hypostyle Hall were used as the canvas for an expansive set of reliefs in which the king encapsulated his military exploits in Syria-Palestine (fig. 49).[66] They were divided into two distinct sections, with an east wing dealing with the southern part of the region and a west one covering places further north. In between was the northern gateway into the Hall, flanked by images of the king smiting his enemies and

FIGURE 60 The north gate of the Hypostyle Hall, flanked by scenes of Sethy I smiting his enemies; these incorporate name rings of the various locations claimed to have been defeated or otherwise dominated by the king.

name rings listing all the places he had allegedly conquered (fig. 60). A further set of name rings from a pair of sphinx bases in the king's memorial temple (page 73) give an even wider range of place names than those at Karnak.[67]

During the decades preceding Sethy I's accession to the throne, a key theme of Egyptian foreign policy had been its relationship with the kingdom of the Hittites in Asia Minor. Although the two powers were subject to a treaty of friendship, perhaps dating back to the middle of the Eighteenth Dynasty, their interests clashed in northern Syria, where Egypt's long-established suzerainty over the various local polities was under pressure from the increasingly powerful Hittites. This is to be seen in a number of items from the Amarna Letters, diplomatic correspondence of the late reign of Amenhotep III and first decade or so of that of Akhenaten, although past assertions that the events covered by these letters constituted a major collapse in Egyptian authority in the region seem certainly to be overstated.[68]

However, relations appear to have been deteriorating during the reign of Tutankhamun, toward the end of which the Hittites made an incursion into the Egyptian-held Amqa area. This was then followed by a much deeper poisoning of relations, a result of the events that had followed the death of Tutankhamun.[69] Then, the king's widow had written to the Hittite king, Shuppiluliuma I, requesting a son of the king to marry her and become the next king of Egypt, following the extinction

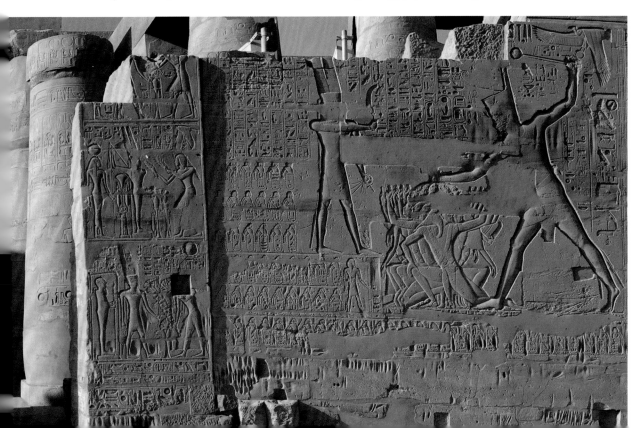

of the male line with the death of her husband. The Egyptian queen stated that she was doing this rather than marry an Egyptian, yet in spite of the implication of a need for rapid action before any 'Egyptian candidate' could consolidate his position, the cautious Shuppiluiuliuma wasted weeks—if not months—sending an emissary to Egypt, and receiving a representative from the queen, before resolving to send his son, Zananza. Had he been sent immediately, with a suitably strong 'escort' to deal with any Egyptian opposition, the prince might have had some chance of gaining power as the queen's spouse; however, he was killed en route and the Egyptian throne was taken by the 'Egyptian candidate'—Ay.

News of Zananza's death led to an immediate Hittite attack on Egyptian forces in northern Syria, in spite of Ay apparently protesting Egypt's innocence in the matter of the prince's death.[70] The attack would, however, have fatal results for the Hittites themselves, since Egyptian prisoners turned out to carry a virulent disease which became endemic and carried off many—including not only Shuppiluiuliuma himself but also his successor as king. This catastrophe clearly distracted the Hittites from prosecuting their war with Egypt with as much vigor as they might have hoped. On the other hand, there is little evidence for the Egyptians having been able to effectively retaliate, retreating from an attempt to take Qadesh—the key strategic stronghold in the region—in Year 7 of the Hittite king Murshili II (the first decade of Horemheb). Amurru and Qadesh were thus in Hittite hands at the time of the accession of Sethy I. Whether this situation had by then been regularized by a treaty is unclear; such an agreement was certainly reached between the two powers sometime during the reigns of Horemheb through Sethy I, but its exact date remains obscure (see further page 59).

However, before becoming embroiled in the far north of his domains, Sethy had to deal with matters much closer to home. These were depicted over the three registers of the eastern wing of the north wall of the Hypostyle Hall, although the topmost is almost entirely destroyed. Each register was devoted to a separate campaign, with the earliest at the bottom. The first episode of the earliest campaign began at the bottom of the northeast wall (fig. 61), the caption relating that in Year 1 a messenger came to tell the king that nomadic Shasu tribal leaders were together in "Khor" (the general Egyptian term for Syria-Palestine) and fighting among themselves. Since this was undermining Egyptian authority in the area, a response was necessary. Its depiction at Karnak featured the king charging his chariot toward a Canaanite fortress, possibly at Gaza (but in any case somewhere around the Egyptian–Palestinian border).

The subsequent episode was placed at the eastern end of the north wall proper (fig. 62), where Sethy was shown receiving homage from a different set of local chieftains—presumably in thanks for intervening in the Shasu civil war that threatened their own

prosperity. There then followed a depiction of the final defeat of the Shasu, and then the king's triumphal procession with his prisoners toward the Egyptian border, marked by a crocodile-infested canal. On the other side of the canal were to be seen a reception committee of Egyptian priests and officials. In its final form the relief showed Crown Prince Rameses walking behind his father's chariot, although as originally carved the figure was that of an official. Finally, the king was shown presenting the booty from the campaign to Amun, the quality of which may suggest that the bulk was a 'thank offering' from the

FIGURE 61 Northeast exterior wall of the Hypostyle Hall, with the first episodes of Sethy I's Shasu (lower register) and Yenoam (upper) campaigns.

Palestinian chieftains, rather than the Shasu themselves. The whole 'campaign' seems thus to have been more a police action combined with an early-reign display of the king and his forces to the inhabitants of southern Palestine than a true military operation. However, the further depictions on the wall seem to have commemorated much more substantive and far-reaching military actions.

The uppermost part of the second register of reliefs is largely lost, with most of the texts—including the date of the events shown. However, a stela from Beth Shan in Palestine (fig. 63) dates the start of the campaign to Year 1, III šmw 10,[71] when it was reported to the king that Beth Shan had been seized by the ruler of Hammath, on the shore of Lake Tiberias. Three armies were sent, one (of Amun) against Hammath, one (of Pre) against Beth Shan, and one (of Seth) against Yenoam (exact location uncertain); all fell within a day of being invested. Perhaps connected with this campaign was the erection of a stela at Tell el-Shihab, some forty kilometers east of Hammath, on the opposite side of the Sea of Galilee.[72]

The attack on Yenoam was shown at the far left end of the second register of the main north wall, after which was placed a depiction of the binding of prisoners, and then their bundling into the royal chariot. The narrative on the register ended with the prisoners being presented to Amun, Mut, and Khonsu. That the campaign extended further northwest is suggested by the fact that directly around the

FIGURE 62 Eastern part of the north exterior wall of the Hypostyle Hall, with the concluding episodes of the Shasu (lower) and Yenoam (upper) campaigns.

corner from the Yenoam battle vignette, on the northeast wall, was carved a depiction of the Lebanese town of "Qader in the land of Henem," shown with its gateposts askew. To the left, Sethy was depicted taking the submission of Lebanese chieftains, who also fell cedars, with the timber to be used to build a new barge for Amun and to provide flagstaves for Amun's temples. To this episode probably belongs a fragment of stela found at the Levantine coastal city of Tyre.[73]

As already noted, only a few fragments of the third register of the eastern part of Sethy's battle tableaux survive, making it impossible to tell which campaigns were once commemorated there, and whether they were also in Syria-Palestine or elsewhere (for example, Nubia: cf. pages 55–58). If the former, they could have included the brief disturbance in a further stela from Beth Shan,[74] or a number of locations mentioned among the name rings accompanying the smiting scenes flanking the gateway at the center of the north wall. These places extend from Gaza in the south up into Upe, where they border the military activities in Amurru and further north into Syria that feature on the west wing of the north wall (fig. 64).

It is uncertain as to the order in which the registers of the west wing are to be read. In most such cases, as on the east wing, they are to be read from the bottom up. However, in this case

FIGURE 63 The first Beth Shan stela (Rockefeller S.884).

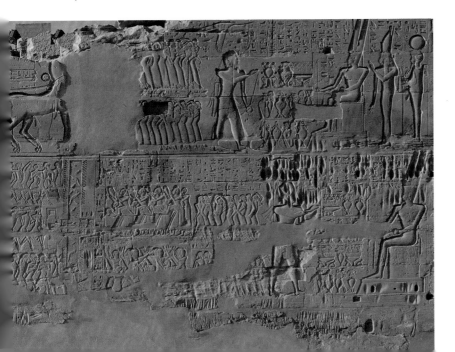

FIGURE 64 Western part of the north exterior wall of the Hypostyle Hall, with the latter episodes of the Hittite (bottom register), Libyan (middle), and Qadesh (top) campaigns. The initial episodes, on the northwest exterior wall, were almost entirely hidden by the construction of the north wall of the First Court under Shoshenq I.

the lowest register records a clash against the Hittites themselves, which most scholars have viewed as more likely to follow, rather than precede, the actions in Syria that occupy the top register. Accordingly, the Sethy I war reliefs have generally been 'read' from bottom to top on the east wing, and then across the top to the west wing, and then down to the 'climax' at the bottom of the west wing.

As on the east wing, the top register is badly damaged, but the first tableau is well preserved, showing the king charging at the north Syrian city of Qadesh. This actually continues a sequence around the corner, on a wall abutting Pylon II, although most of the tableau in

question is obscured by its juncture with the enclosure wall of the First Court, added some four centuries later by Shoshenq I. This scene presumably commemorated an action leading up to the attack on Qadesh, probably in the Amurru region to the southwest. Sethy I's conquest of Qadesh is confirmed by the discovery there of a fragment of stela showing the king before a range of gods;[75] indeed, its crudity may suggest that it was made straight after the capture of the city to cement the victory.[76] Nevertheless, Qadesh would fairly soon return to Hittite suzerainty, as Sethy's son Rameses II had later to fight a famous battle in an (unsuccessful) attempt to recover it for Egypt.

Sometime after his Qadesh campaign, assuming that our understanding of the order of registers at Karnak is correct, Sethy had occasion to fight on Egypt's western border against the Tjehenu Libyans. However, the tableaux of the king fighting in his chariot and on foot seem fairly generic, as are those of the marching of prisoners toward a presentation to the Theban triad. The nature of the campaign is thus obscure, but it is worth noting that a Libyan threat would grow over the coming decades, culminating in an attempted invasion under Sethy's grandson, Merenptah.[77]

In the meantime, the Hittites had clearly reacted to the loss of Qadesh, since the lowest register of the west wing was used to depict a war against the "vile land of the Hittites." As was the case higher up the wall, the first episode, on the northwestern wall, is now hidden under the abutting First Courtyard wall of Shoshenq I, but it is followed by one showing Sethy charging into a defeated mass of Hittites. Unlike other parts of Sethy's war reliefs, no geographical data are provided in the visible reliefs. Nevertheless, the succeeding scenes show the escorting of Hittite prisoners southward and their presentation to the Theban triad and Maat. It is possible that Sethy's success against the Hittites was aided by the latter being distracted by an Assyrian invasion of Hanigalbat, the rump of the former kingdom of Mitanni, and hitherto under Hittite suzerainty. Hanigalbat would later revert to Hittite control, with its forces fighting on their side at Rameses II's battle of Qadesh.

Aside from his military activities in Syria-Palestine, at least one campaign is known to have taken place in Nubia. This is evidenced by stelae from Sai and Amara West,[78] dated to Year 8[79] [...] *prt* 20, which report that an expedition was sent southward following a report of a rebellion in Irem, an area of Upper Nubia that seems to have lain beyond the limit of formal Egyptian control. The resulting combat lasted for a week, at the end of which six strategic wells had been seized and over four hundred of the 'rebels' and their families captured and taken northward, presumably to serve as forced laborers.

The King's Men

Although nominally an omnipotent and omniprescient divine ruler, the king's actual government of course relied on a large team of state officials, together with those from the royal household as well as senior members of the principal priesthoods. Since the Old Kingdom the head of the government had been the vizier, an office which became split into northern and southern posts during the Eighteenth Dynasty. Two holders of the vizieral title are known from the reign of Sethy I, Nebamun and Paser (fig. 66),[80] but there remains some debate over whether they were respectively northern and southern viziers[81] or whether they successively occupied the southern role.[82]

Of the two, Nebamun is known only from a statue from Abydos, a statue base from Karnak, and a mention in an accounts papyrus.[83] Paser, whose career continued under Rameses II and culminated in his appointment (like his father—see below) as high priest

FIGURE 65 The Overseer of the Harem Hormin rewarded by Sethy I; from Saqqara tomb LS29 (Louvre C.213).

FIGURE 66 Relief, cut down into a stela, showing Sethy I and a vizier (whose name is lost) before the deified Eighteenth Dynasty king, Amenhotep I, and his mother, Queen Ahmes-Nefertiry; from Deir el-Medina (Turin S.6189+6193).

of Amun,[84] is attested under Sethy I by a reward scene, in other texts, in his tomb chapel (TT106), and by his representation in a tomb relief of the Deir el-Medina workman Ameneminet.[85] Regarding heads of government departments, two overseers of granaries, Nefersekheru and Sieset, have been placed during Sethy's reign, as have a number of members of the court, the royal household (fig. 65), and the army.[86] A messenger to every foreign land, Ashahebused, is also known from the records of a number of expeditions to the turquoise mines of Sinai, one of them during Year 8.[87]

Doubtless many of the officials known from Rameses II's earliest years began their service under his father, but in only a few cases, such as the handful noted above, do we have clear evidence for this. One further example is the high priest of Amun Bakenkhonsu, who served in this role late in the reign of Rameses II, but whose autobiographical inscription mentions that early in his career he spent eleven years as a stable master to Sethy I.[88]

3 THE MANSION OF MILLIONS OF YEARS AND THE HOUSE OF ETERNITY

O mitted from the monuments described in the previous chapter have been two that were intended to service Sethy I's eternal wellbeing. While the Abydos complex was clearly intended to serve the king's eternal fusion with Osiris, it was on the Theban West Bank that his body was to rest, and where lay the principal place that his spirit would continue to interface with this world.

As noted in chapter 2 (pages 57–58), the latest dated monument of Sethy I comes from IV *šmw* in Year 9, the same year that saw the quarry order for a number of obelisks and colossi that appear to have been finished under Rameses II (page 55). If the interpretation of the latter situation is indeed correct, it would imply that Sethy died within at most two years of the order to commence quarrying. Given that the accession day of Rameses II is generally agreed to have been III *šmw* 27,[1] and Sethy's own may have been III *šmw* 24,[2] it would follow that Sethy I reigned for three days short of ten or eleven full years.[3] The latter would fit in well with the statement of Bakenkhonsu (previous page) that he served as a stable master under Sethy I for eleven years, his transfer to the Amun priesthood coming with the accession of Rameses II. It may also be noted that the highest date mentioned on wine jar dockets from the king's tomb is in Year 8.[4]

Since the earliest times, the ideal Egyptian tomb had comprised two distinct elements: an accessible offering place where the worlds of the living and the dead met and where sustenance and prayers could be delivered as part of a mortuary cult, and the actual burial place, usually subterranean and intended to be sealed for eternity.[5] The implementation of this scheme of course varied according to the wealth and social status of the deceased, thus ranging from a simple grave, with no focus for a cult beyond the ground above the filled grave, through a monumental cult installation, associated with an architecturally and artistically elaborate burial complex.

Royal examples usually represented the peak of elaboration and scale, although exceptions exist.[6] During the Old Kingdom, kings' sepulchers comprised pyramids placed above the burial chamber, with a mortuary temple on the eastern side, connected to a valley building on the boundary of the desert and the cultivated flood plain of the Nile. The mortuary temple had at its innermost point the actual offering place, initially flanked by a pair of stelae bearing the king's names, but later taking the form of a false door stela, a very concrete manifestation of the concept of the temple acting as a boundary between the worlds.

As time went by, the temple became larger in proportion to the pyramid itself, and also more elaborate, with increasing proportions of the wall surfaces occupied by decoration. Themes employed included both those found in the chapels of contemporary private tombs, such as food production, hunting, and fishing, and themes appropriate to a divine king, such as interactions with the gods and 'historical' scenes, in particular relating to warfare. Although details are often obscured by the damaged state of all known such temples, there seems to have been a transition from 'secular' themes to more sacred ones the deeper a visitor ventured into the complex. By the beginning of the Fifth Dynasty, decoration had come to extend all the way down the causeway and into the valley building.

This basic scheme was revived at the beginning of the Twelfth Dynasty and, with detail variations, continued in use until the cessation of the construction of monumental royal tombs during the Thirteenth Dynasty. Kings' tombs of the later Second Intermediate Period were very small, brick-lined structures with no surviving traces of superstructure being built at Abydos, while at Thebes during the Seventeenth Dynasty they comprised a small pyramid and adjoining chapel, but with the actual burial place at the bottom of a rock-cut shaft some distance away.

This separation of the body from its hitherto customary close proximity to the offering place was maintained when a full-size pyramid was built once more, by Ahmose I at Abydos. In this case, the mortuary temple lay directly adjacent to the pyramid, but the subterranean tomb itself was cut a kilometer to the west, with a further temple two hundred meters beyond it.

The pyramid was abandoned altogether under Amenhotep I, who erected a mortuary chapel at Deir el-Bahari but had his tomb over a kilometer to the north, among the wadis behind the Dra Abu'l-Naga hills, which had been the location of the Seventeenth Dynasty royal tombs.[7] This pattern of a pyramidless complex, with wide separation of the offering and burial elements, would continue for the rest of the New Kingdom, with the tombs themselves soon concentrated in a set of wadis west of Deir el-Bahari, now known as the Valley of the Kings (fig. 67).

The offering places associated with these tombs were mainly constructed along the edge of the desert, all broadly oriented toward the Karnak complex on the opposite

bank of the river. Aside from the omission of an associated pyramid, their conception differed significantly from the mortuary temples of the Old and Middle Kingdoms. Rather than being solely focused on the dead king's own cult, the new type of temple (nowadays dubbed a 'memorial temple') was divided among three separate foci. First, on the central axis lay a shrine dedicated to a form of Amun specific to the temple in question; second, to the north of the Amun shrine stood an open-court altar dedicated to the sun god Re; third, to the south of the Amun shrine was the shrine of the dead king, with an adjacent shrine dedicated to the king's father.

The best-preserved Eighteenth Dynasty example of this kind of temple, and also one of the very earliest, is that of Hatshepsut at Deir el-Bahari. This also included further chapels to Hathor and Anubis and followed a dramatically terraced design, probably dictated by the topography of its location. This was remote from the desert-edge location typical of most memorial temples, and as a result the temple had a causeway leading over a kilometer west to the last known

FIGURE 67 Panorama of the Valley of the Kings, showing the location of KV17, the tomb of Sethy I.

example of a valley building. The decoration of the temple followed the same themes as had been established back in the Old Kingdom, the female king being shown fishing and fowling in the marshes, associating with the gods, and presiding over events such as a trading expedition to the Red Sea country of Punt, as well as the transport of obelisks from Aswan to Karnak.

The detail of the subsequent evolution of memorial temples down to the beginning of the Nineteenth Dynasty is obscured by the poor preservation of subsequent examples, which are in the main demolished down to floor level or below, leaving many details of even the plan unclear.

The Memorial Temple

Fortunately, Sethy I's memorial temple is far better preserved than its immediate precursors (figs. 68, 69).[8] It was built some way north of the main group of New Kingdom memorial temples, to place it directly opposite Karnak, and at the end of a canal that formed part of the processional route for Amun's image during the Beautiful Festival of the Valley. The latter involved a progress across the Nile, and then along the front of the Theban necropolis to the climax of the festival at Deir el-Bahari.

FIGURE 68 The inner part of the memorial temple of Sethy I at Qurna.

The temple was fronted by two brick pylons with stone gateways, but both are largely destroyed. A pair of colossal sphinxes stood just beyond Pylon I, although only their bases survive, inscribed with a long list of foreign name rings (cf. page 59). To the south of the court was built a palace, a feature apparently first found in the memorial temple of Horemheb,[9] and this would be an element of all later New Kingdom memorial temples, generally following the basic plan found in the Sethy I temple.

The main body of the temple lay at the back of the second courtyard, fronted by a portico of lotus-bundle columns. The portico, like much of the temple, was left undecorated at Sethy's death and only adorned under Rameses II, with tableaux depicting the Feast of the Valley. On the main axis (of Amun), the portico opened onto a six-pillared hypostyle hall (A, fig. 70), with two small chapels on either side. This part of the temple had been decorated by Sethy I in raised relief, the chapels being consecrated to the royal cult. Chapel B was dedicated to the deified king, C to the royal bark, and D and E to the king's assimilation with Osiris and with Amun, respectively. The walls of the hall were in the process of decoration when Sethy died, with the result that some scenes were completed under Rameses II and thus bore his names rather than those of his father.

Beyond the hall lay the cult area of Amun (F and G), flanked by chapels of Mut (H) and Khonsu (I). The Amun suite comprised two pillared rooms, each with subsidiaries. The first pillared element (F) included a pedestal to support the bark of the god during the Feast of the Valley, with the bark depicted on both side walls (fig. 71). The inner room (G), with square rather than cylindrical pillars, was adorned with a range of images of Sethy in the presence of the gods (fig. 72); all of this part of the temple had been decorated prior to Sethy's death.

In contrast, the Re complex (J, fig. 73) was left entirely for Rameses II to decorate, which he did not actually do for some two

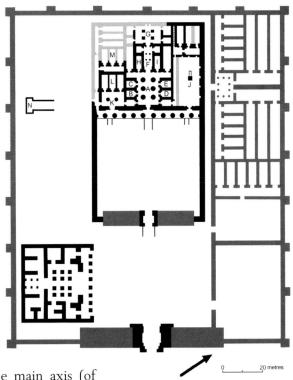

FIGURE 69 Plan of the memorial temple of Sethy I.

FIGURE 70 The hypostyle hall of the memorial temple of Sethy I, looking west into the Amun-chapel.

decades, as is shown by the spelling of his nomen, which was changed soon after his Year 20. The exterior surfaces of the temple were also decorated at this time, as were a number of other hitherto unadorned areas.

Decoratively intermediate between these two extremes were the rooms in the southern half of the temple (K–M), where work begun by Sethy I was continued and completed by Rameses II. As in earlier memorial temples, these were dedicated to the funerary cult of the owner of the temple and to his father. However, unlike in the temple of Hatshepsut, where the chapel of Thutmose I was considerably smaller than that of the king herself, the installation of Rameses I was of exactly the same size as that of Sethy. It was also in the more prominent position, accessible directly from the main portico, while that of Sethy lay behind it, reached by an awkward route. This may simply reflect the respect that Sethy had for his father—or that

FIGURE 71 The bark room of the Amun-chapel.

FIGURE 72 The inner hall of the Amun-chapel.

FIGURE 73 The solar court of Re-Horakhty.

Rameses may never have completed his own temple, leaving his chapel in his son's temple as his sole funerary installation at Thebes.

Indeed, it is possible that Sethy I's memorial temple had originally been founded as Rameses I's intended establishment. The temple shows signs of having slightly different axes for each of its three dedicatory components, with a number of other discontinuities in the structure, including the use of limestone for the lower elements of the inner part of the Amun complex.[10] In addition, various parts of the temple display areas of erasure of earlier decoration. On this basis, it seems not unlikely that the core of the temple had been begun and partly decorated by Rameses I, but that the whole building was then recast and redecorated from scratch by Sethy—but retaining Rameses's intended funerary chapel on the scale originally meant for him.[11]

These royal funerary chapels were accessed via a two-pillared vestibule (K, fig. 74). This had been decorated under Rameses II, partly soon after his accession in raised relief and partly later in sunk relief.[12] The two kings' installations each comprised three rooms in parallel. In that of Rameses I, only the central one (L) was actually decorated under Sethy I. This bore a double false-door stela at its end, showing the Osiride Rameses I, and side walls that showed Sethy I both before the bark of Amun and anointing Rameses I. The other

FIGURE 74 The main axis of the mortuary chapel of Rameses I.

two rooms were decorated under Rameses II in sunk relief, with him offering to the Theban triad.

Sethy I's own installation (L) lay directly behind that of his father, accessed by a corridor running along the south side of the latter. However, although its vestibule is largely intact (fig. 75), the three chapels are now essentially destroyed (fig. 76). It is thus unknown whether any of them had been decorated during their author's lifetime. On the other hand, the vestibule was certainly adorned by Rameses II, albeit including some images of Sethy I, offering to Amun and to Osiris.

A small 'sacred lake' lay to the south of the temple, within the overall enclosure wall (N). The latter, in brick and strengthened with buttresses, was an innovation of Sethy I, as such walls are not known from earlier memorial temples, and was also employed at his Abydos

FIGURE 75 The vestibule of the mortuary chapel of Sethy I himself, showing
the entrances to the three sanctuaries. The room was decorated by Rameses II.

FIGURE 76 In contrast to the parallel chapel of Rameses I, the three sanctuaries of that
of Sethy I were almost entirely destroyed, leaving just the lowest courses of masonry.

complex. Between the temple and the northern enclosure wall lay a large set of brick storerooms, to house produce derived from the estates endowed to support the operation of the temple.

The Tomb

As already noted, the Valley of the Kings had become the actual burial place of the kings of Egypt early in the Eighteenth Dynasty; except for a brief hiatus during the Amarna Period, the Valley would be used for all kingly burials down to the last years of the Twentieth Dynasty. The first king to have been buried there seems to have been Thutmose I, although there remains debate as to the identity of his original tomb, as his body was moved at least once following his death, ending up in a new sarcophagus made by Thutmose III for his final Eighteenth Dynasty reburial in tomb KV38.[13] It has been proposed that his original tomb was KV20, a sinuous set of galleries unlike any later king's tomb in the Valley. This was ultimately occupied by Hatshepsut, whose burial chamber was decorated with the first of the series of "Books of the Underworld," which formed the basis of the decoration for all later orthodox royal tombs.[14]

Kings' tombs of the later Old Kingdom had been adorned with the Pyramid Texts, a compilation of spells relating to the royal afterlife. These evolved into the Middle Kingdom Coffin Texts, which are known from private coffins but do not appear in the only known Middle Kingdom king's coffin, that of the Thirteenth Dynasty Hor; nor do any Middle Kingdom kings' tombs have any decoration. Thus, the appearance of decoration in Hatshepsut's burial chamber marked a new beginning in the conception of the Egyptian royal tomb.

The composition found in this tomb was the Book of *Amduat* (*imy-dw3t*: "What is in the Underworld"), which depicted and narrated the journey of the sun god through the netherworld, from his 'death' at sunset to his rebirth at sunrise. This journey was divided into twelve 'hours,' during which time the god and his companions faced and defeated hazards and enemies, while also bringing light to the denizens of the region of the dead. The underlying conception seems to have been that the dead king would share in the sun's journey and then its rebirth at dawn. One of the earliest, and most complete, copies of the *Amduat*, that of Thutmose III in his tomb KV34 (fig. 77), contained frequent mentions of the king, but these all but disappear from the redactions found in later royal tombs (and much later also in private papyri). The tomb of Thutmose III also contained, on its pillars, parts of another new composition, the Litany of Re, which invoked the sun god in his myriad names and forms. Curiously, this work was not again used in the decoration of a royal tomb until the Nineteenth Dynasty.

FIGURE 77 The burial chamber of Thutmose III in KV34, showing the king's quartzite sarcophagus and the cursive version of the Book of *Amduat* (shown as if written on papyrus) that was typical of pre-Amarna kings' tombs.

Apart from an extensive list of deities in the antechamber of KV34, the *Amduat* remained the sole 'Book' used to decorate royal tombs down to the reign of Amenhotep III (WV22), although increasingly supplemented by depictions of the king before the gods. After a break caused by the religious revolution of Akhenaten, orthodoxy returned to royal tombs with that of Tutankhamun (KV62). However, the burial chambers of Tutankhamun and Ay (WV23) contained only the beginning of the First Hour of the *Amduat*, otherwise being adorned with images of the king and the gods, alongside other tableaux unique to those two tombs (for example, fig. 5). Presumably the view was taken that the presence of the first element of the *Amduat* would magically generate the remainder, abbreviated versions of the Second and Sixth Hours (only), also being inscribed on the third of the four gilded shrines that surrounded the sarcophagus of Tutankhamun.

While the small size of the burial chambers of the tombs in question could explain the drastic abbreviation of the *Amduat* in these cases, a wholly contiguous *Amduat* would never again appear on the walls of a royal tomb. Furthermore, the next king's tomb, that of Horemheb (KV57), omitted the *Amduat* altogether, his burial chamber instead being decorated with a truncated version of a new composition, the Book of Gates, which also appeared in even more abbreviated form in the tiny burial chamber of Rameses I (fig. 12). The Gates resembled the *Amduat* in being built around the sun god's nocturnal voyage and being divided into twelve hours, but featured prominent gates between each hour, a different set of divine and human figures, and in

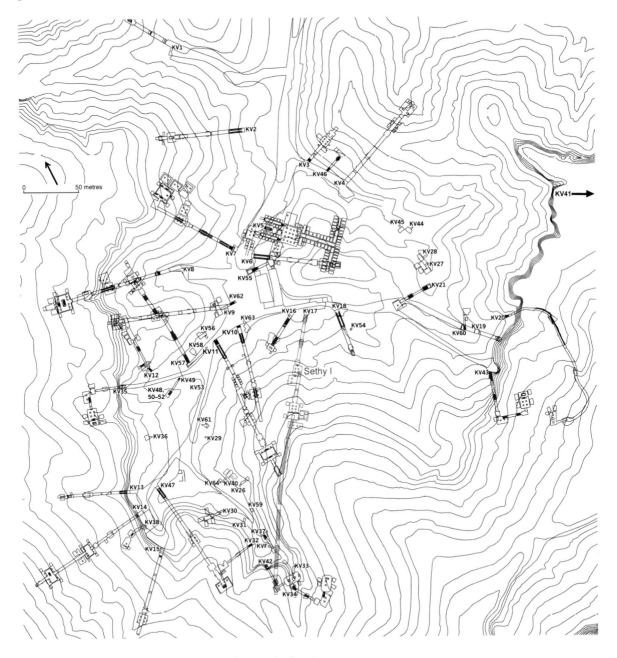

FIGURE 78 Map of the Valley of the Kings, showing the location of the tomb of Sethy I, including the extent of its lower passage.

FIGURE 79 Plan and sections of the tomb of Sethy I.

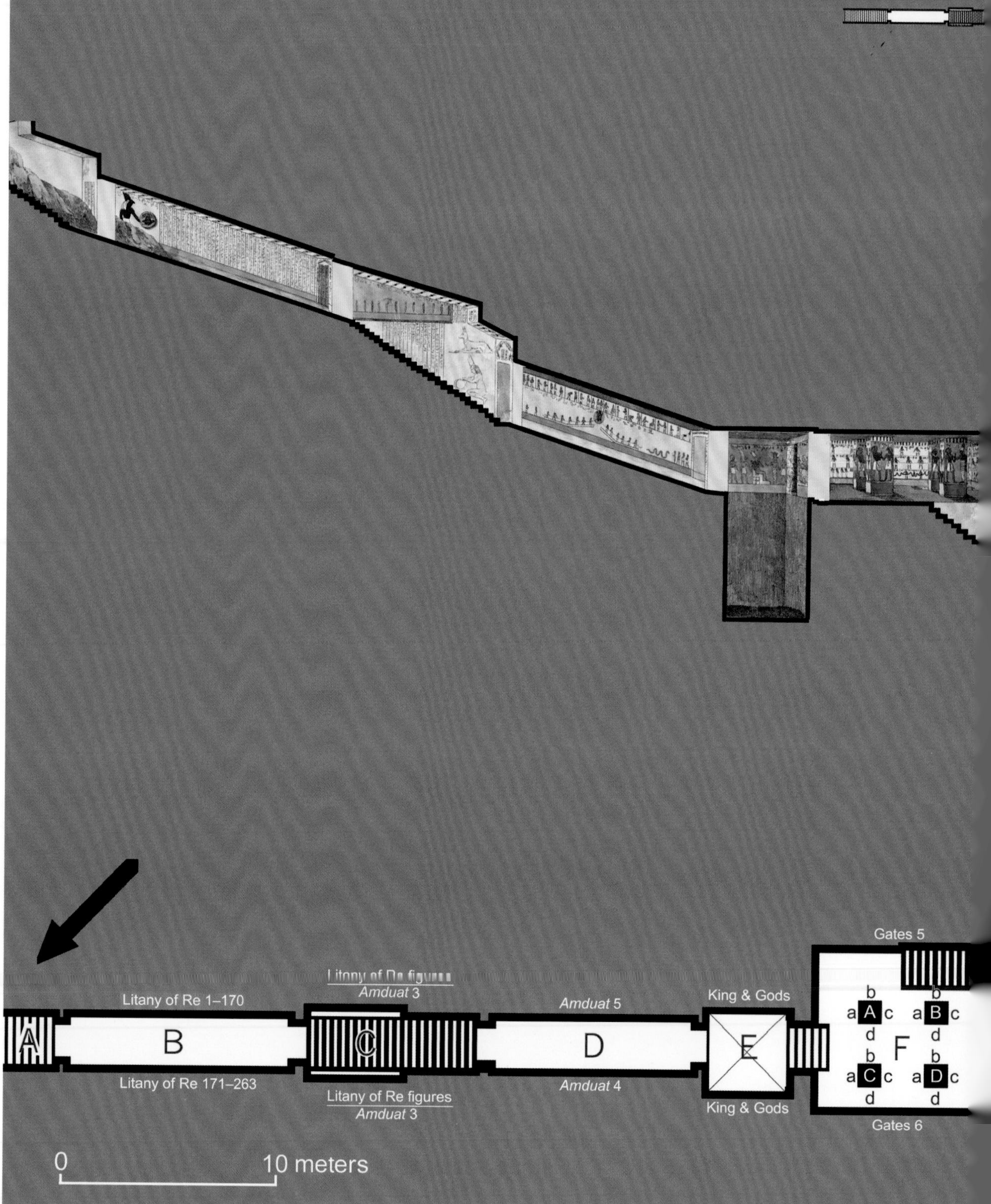

Litany of Re 1–170

Litany of Re figures
Amduat 3

Amduat 5

King & Gods

Gates 5

A
B
C
D
E
F

Litany of Re 171–263

Litany of Re figures
Amduat 3

Amduat 4

King & Gods

Gates 6

0   10 meters

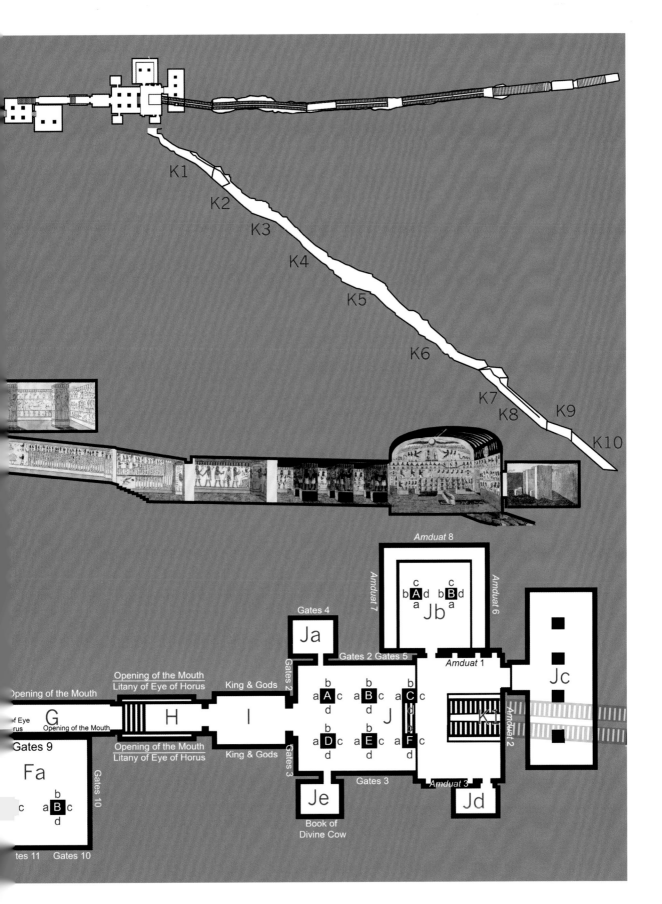

K1
K2
K3
K4
K5
K6
K7
K8
K9
K10

Amduat 8

Amduat 7   Amduat 6

c   c
b A d b B d
a   a
Jb

Gates 4

Ja

Gates 2 Gates 5

Jc

Gates 2

Opening of the Mouth
Litany of Eye of Horus

Amduat 1

Opening of the Mouth

King & Gods

b   b   b
a A c a B c a C c c
d   d
of Eye   G   H   I   J   K1
rus   Opening of the Mouth   Amduat 2

Gates 9   b   b   b
a D c a E c a F c c
d   d

Gates 3

Opening of the Mouth
Litany of Eye of Horus

King & Gods

Amduat 3

Fa

Gates 10

Gates 3

Amduat 3

b
c a B c
d

Je

Jd

Book of
Divine Cow

tes 11   Gates 10

its earliest versions included the Judgement Hall of the Dead in its itinerary; later (from the time of Sethy I), this was replaced by a tableau of the king before Osiris (see fig. 86).

Until the Amarna Period, New Kingdom kings' tombs had been cut with a 'bent' axis, with a right-angled turn around their midpoint, usually marked by an upper pillared hall. However, the first structurally complete post-Amarna sepulcher, that of Horemheb, abandoned this feature in favor of a slight lateral shift of the main axis following the upper pillared hall. Otherwise, however, the basic form of the tomb continued a pattern established under Thutmose III, with a deep shaft between the initial stairs and corridors and the upper pillared hall, and a burial chamber equipped with subsidiary rooms. Since the time of Amenhotep II (KV35), the burial chamber had been rectangular and comprised a six-pillared outer section, followed by a sunken crypt in which the sarcophagus lay, surrounded by wooden shrines, examples of which were found in Tutankhamun's tomb. An antechamber had been added directly outside the burial chamber under Amenhotep III.

Horemheb's tomb was also innovative in that it was the first tomb in the Valley of the Kings to be decorated in carved relief, rather than simply flat paint. This had a number of important implications, as it meant that the decoration would take far longer to execute and also required a completely different skill mix among those constructing the tomb. The latter may have been the cause of a major expansion of the workmen's community at Deir el-Medina in Year 7 of Horemheb's reign, while the dislocation of decorative timescales may explain why only part of his tomb had received its full decoration by the king's death.[15]

The design established by Horemheb had presumably been intended to be used for Rameses I's tomb (KV16), but, as already noted (page 14), it had to be truncated after its second staircase, a makeshift burial chamber being cut where the second corridor should have begun, with no question of employing anything more than painted decoration. Although not far from Horemheb's tomb, the location chosen for KV16 differed from those of most earlier kings' tombs (fig. 78). These had generally lain at the bottom of clefts in the rock, with the intent that all traces of their entrances might be obliterated by debris carried over the clifftops by periodic flash floods (cf. page 129). However, by the beginning of the Nineteenth Dynasty, all such sites had apparently been taken, KV16 being cut into the flank of a low hill.

Sethy I began his tomb, now numbered KV17,[16] directly next to that of his father, but he was able to not only implement Horemheb's full architectural and decorative conception, but also greatly expand the latter aspect. This was apparent from the very entrance (fig. 116). As noted, decoration of royal tombs had previously been restricted to the burial chamber and possibly one or two antechambers: in that of Horemheb just the burial chamber, the antechamber, and the room containing the shaft had decoration. In Sethy I's tomb, however, even the lintel of the doorway at the bottom of the initial stairway (A) bore the king's cartouches, flanked by images of the goddess Maat. The doorjambs also bore his names and titles, heralding a decorative scheme that extended into almost every corridor, stairway, and room of the tomb (fig. 79). Just inside this doorway were installed a pair of inwardly opening doors.[17] These do not seem to have been part of the original plan and may have been fitted to temporarily secure the tomb during the run-up to the funeral.

Immediately inside this entrance, the king was greeted on the left by Re-Horakhty (fig. 80). This tableau was followed by the beginning of the text of the Litany of Re, which extended down the whole left wall of corridor B (for designations of spaces within the tomb, see fig. 79) and continued on the right wall, starting directly inside the doorway of the tomb. The ceiling of this corridor was painted blue and adorned with the images of vultures and the king's cartouches and titles, on a background of yellow stars (fig. 81). The images that formed part of the Litany were placed in niches that flanked stairway C, while the text of the Third Hour of the *Amduat* occupied the lower halves of the stairway's walls and also its ceiling, where the text was painted in yellow on blue. The carving of the *Amduat* text on the walls had not been completed, much of it still being in its black ink preliminary drawing when work on it was abandoned.

The outer lintel of the gate between the stairway and corridor D bore a winged figure of Maat, the inner tableau being a replica of that at the entrance to the tomb, with Maat extending her wings in protection around the king's cartouches (fig. 82). This inner lintel was at the same level as the unfinished *Amduat* material in the preceding element of the tomb and was never carved, only painted. Corridor D was decorated on both walls

FIGURE 80 Start of the left wall of corridor B, showing Re-Horakhty welcoming the king to the Underworld.

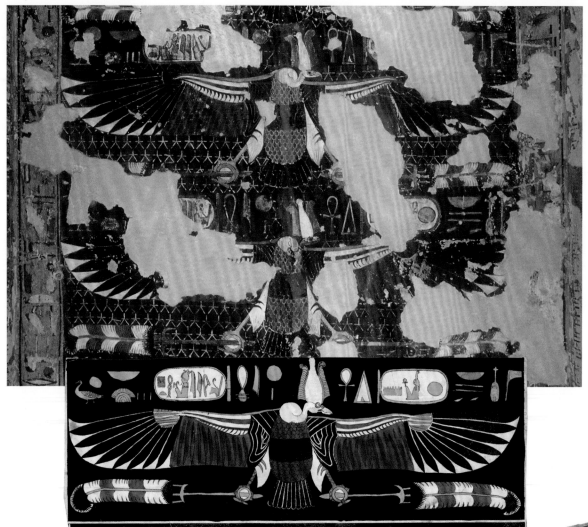

FIGURE 81 Ceiling of corridor B, showing current state and a copy made in 1818.

FIGURE 82 Gateway between stairway C and corridor D, featuring three representations of the goddess Maat. The lintel of the inner gate is painted only, while the texts and vignettes on the walls at the same level were mainly only sketched in ink and never completed.

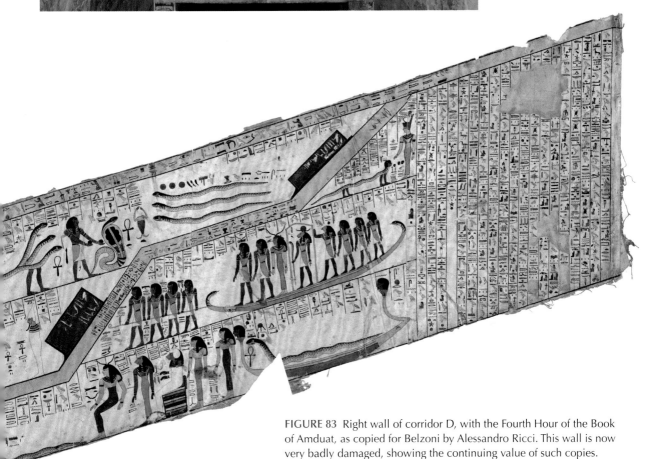

FIGURE 83 Right wall of corridor D, with the Fourth Hour of the Book of Amduat, as copied for Belzoni by Alessandro Ricci. This wall is now very badly damaged, showing the continuing value of such copies.

FIGURE 84 Detail of the decoration of the left wall of well room E, showing the gray background that distinguishes it from the rest of the tomb.

with sections of the *Amduat*, the left wall with the Fifth Hour, the right with the end of the Third Hour and the whole of the Fourth (fig. 83). The ceiling was painted blue with yellow stars—a scheme used throughout the rest of the tomb, with the exception of the vault of the crypt of the burial chamber (see page 99).

Beyond corridor D lay the well room (E), the walls adorned with depictions of the king in the presence of the gods, and its floor cut away into a deep shaft, with two rough rooms at the bottom. The decoration had originally extended over a blocked doorway in the far wall, clearly intended to deceive and frustrate robbers, who had to both cross the void and break through the blocking: ancient documents call this room in a tomb *t3 wšḥt isq*, the "Hall of Hindering" or "Waiting" (see below). Nevertheless, robbers did succeed in doing both (see page 126 for the state of this part of the tomb when entered in 1817).

It has been debated whether the shaft had further practical and/or theological significance(s), in particular the protection of the tomb from infiltrating floodwater (cf. page 129) and as a symbolic access point to the underworld.[18] Interestingly, the well room seems to have been the first part of the tomb to have been decorated, to judge from the style and proportions of the figures, which resemble those in the tombs of Horemheb and Rameses I more than those of Sethy I elsewhere in the tomb. Their gray background also ties this room to the earlier tombs (fig. 84), while the orthography used here for Sethy's names also differs from those generally used in the tomb.[19] All this would suggest that the original plan was that KV17 should follow the more sparse decorative plan of earlier tombs, in which the well room was the outermost decorated chamber, before the ultimate scheme of decoration was adopted.

Our knowledge of the ancient name for the well room comes from a number of ancient sources, consisting of ostraca and papyri deriving from the Nineteenth and Twentieth Dynasties.[20] These also give the following names to the preceding elements of the tomb:

Stairway A: *p3 sṯ3-nṯr (tpy) n w3t šw*
             The (First) God's Passage of the Way of Shu

Corridor B: *p3 sṯ3-nṯr nty r mḥ 2*
             The Second God's Passage, or
             p3 sṯ3-nṯr nty n Rʿ
             The God's Passage of Re

Stairway C: *p3 sṯ3-nṯr nty r-mḥ 3*
             The Third God's Passage

niches: *n3ḥ ḥmy nty ḥtpw i3bt/iwnt imw*
             Sanctuaries in Which the Gods of the East/West Rest

Corridor D: *p3 sṯ3-nṯr nty r-mḥ 3*
             The Third God's Passage

The alternate designation of corridor B may reflect the fact that its decoration in KV17 and other tombs comprised the Litany of Re.

FIGURE 85 Left-hand entrance wall of chamber F, with the beginning of the Fifth Hour of the Book of Gates.

FIGURE 86 The king before Osiris, between the Fifth and Sixth Hours of the Book of Gates, on the rear wall of chamber F. The rectangle in the center shows the results of experimental cleaning. For a nineteenth-century AD view of the scene as one of masonic initiation, see pages 138–39.

The well room led into the upper pillared hall (F). The main ancient designation of this space was *t3 wsḫt mrḫt*, the "Chariot Hall," presumably reflecting that this was where the chariots that formed part of New Kingdom royal (and some other) funerary equipment were placed.[21] Its walls bore principally the Fourth, Fifth, and Sixth Hours of the Book of Gates (fig. 85), including the scene of the king before Osiris that had now replaced the Judgement Hall depiction used in the tomb of Horemheb (fig. 86). The roof of the hall was supported by four pillars, the faces of each showing the king before a different deity (fig. 87).

A further hall (Fa) lay beyond, in this case with two columns, again with images of the king before deities; however, in this case the walls shifted to the *Amduat*, showing the Ninth, Tenth, and Eleventh Hours (fig. 88). Unlike most of the rest of the tomb, but like parts of the lower walls of stairway C, the decoration of this hall had only ever been drawn out in ink and never carved, suggesting that the chamber was a late addition to the design of the tomb. In support of this is the fact that no corresponding chamber exists in any earlier tomb. Work had been begun in cutting into the right wall for a niche or further chamber, but this was never completed.

The unfinished state of the decoration here and in other similar situations (including in Horemheb's burial chamber) provides a useful window on the way the ancient workmen went about their tasks.

FIGURE 87 Face c of column D in chamber D, showing the king before Selqet.

Thus, after a wall had been quarried, a thin layer of plaster was laid over the surface, upon which the decorating scheme was laid out in red ink. After this, the definitive line work, including corrections where necessary, was drawn in black ink, which formed the

FIGURE 88 Chamber Fa, showing the drawn, but not yet carved, decoration, that of the wall comprising the Ninth through Eleventh Hours of the Book of Gates.

basis for sculptors to cut away the background and model the raised elements, which would finally be painted to complete the work.

It was at hall F that the axis of the tomb shifted to the left (as previously found in the tomb of Horemheb), an undecorated stairway, originally filled in and paved over, descending from the floor of the hall. This sealed exit may account for an alternate name given to hall F in ancient times: "Another Hall of Repelling Enemies" *(kt wsḫt dr sbiw)*. At the bottom of the stairway, the deep doorjambs each depicted the king before Hathor, presenting him with a *mnit* necklace (fig. 89). Beyond these scenes began a long sequence related to the Opening of the Mouth, starting with an image of the dead king in front of an offering table on the left wall (fig. 90). Before him is shown the Iunmutef priest, responsible for the ritual, a series of depictions of which then unfolded down the whole length of the left wall of corridor G, most of the right wall, and in the inset upper parts of both walls of the shallow staircase H (fig. 91). The lower parts

FIGURE 89 The left and right jambs of the entrance to corridor G, removed by Rosellini and Champollion (cf. page 142 and fig. 129) (Florence 2468; Louvre B.7).

of the walls of staircase H were adorned with the Litany of the Eye of Horus, which extended into the bottom end of the right wall of corridor G, which also accommodated a list of offerings.

Conceptually, corridor G seems to have been regarded as the beginning of a new section of the tomb, as implied by one of the ancient terms for this passage, *p3 ky st3-ntr qr tpy n wpt*, "Another First God's Passage of the Sun's Nocturnal Zenith," and *p3 ky st3-ntr r-mh 2*, "Another Second God's Passage," for staircase H. At the this point, a doorway, originally closed by a single-leaf, inward-opening wooden door, led into the tomb's antechamber, or *t3 wsht m3't*, "Hall of Truth" (I, fig. 92). This room followed the same basic decorative scheme as the well room, but on a larger scale, with the king before a wide range of deities, in some cases making offerings to them (figs. 93, 130). Beyond, a final wooden door once closed the entrance to the burial chamber itself, a room named *pr n nbw/wsht nty htp.tw m-im*, the "House of Gold / Hall in Which One Rests" (J, fig. 94).

The roof of the outer part of the burial chamber was supported by six pillars (fig. 95), the pillar faces on the axial route through the hall all being adorned with depictions of the primordial genii, the Souls of Pe (canine-headed, on the left [J/A–Cd]) and Nekhen (raptor-headed, on the right [J/D–Fb]). The rest of the pillar faces each showed the king

FIGURE 90 The beginning of the Opening of the Mouth sequence on the left wall of corridor G, with the king seated before an offering table and the sem-priest, who is repeated above, facing the opposite direction and initiating the ritual.

before a deity (fig. 96), except for the first pillar on the left, whose outer face (J/Aa) showed the Iunmutef priest, who had previously undertaken the Opening of the Mouth of the king in G and H.

The decoration of the walls of the left-hand half of the pillared part of the burial chamber began with the Second Hour of the Book of Gates, continuing with the Fifth Hour. Halfway along, a door opened into chamber Ja, whose walls were adorned with the Fourth Hour (fig. 97). The right-hand half of the pillared space bore the Third Hour of

FIGURE 91 Episodes 45–47 of the Opening of the Mouth, on the right wall of corridor G.

FIGURE 92 View through chamber I into corridor/stair H.

FIGURE 93 Right-hand wall of chamber I, showing the king before Hathor, Horus, Isis, and Anubis, showing the modern state of the wall. Some parts have lost their color entirely through wet squeezing, some have it obscured by the results of Belzoni's wax casting (see page 128), and others have been the subject of experimental cleaning.

FIGURE 94 View from chamber J back into chamber I, showing repairs undertaken by Howard Carter, early in the twentieth century.

FIGURE 95
View from
the crypt of
chamber J into
its pillared
portion.

FIGURE 96 Two pillars of chamber J were badly damaged or destroyed early in the nineteenth century, face a of pillar B, with the king before Osiris, being taken to Berlin by Lepsius (ÄM2058; left). Pillar E was almost entirely destroyed, including this face showing a ram-headed Ptah-Sokar before the king, preserved here in a 'yellow' copy (see page 138), ultimately derived from Ricci (right).

the Gates, while its subsidiary room, Je, contained the Book of the Divine Cow (fig. 98), a composition previously found only on one of the shrines of Tutankhamun and, while later included in the tombs of Rameses II and III ([KV7 and KV11] and briefly excerpted in that of Rameses VI [KV9]), far less widely employed than other Books of the Underworld. It described a rebellion of mankind against the sun god, and his punishment of it; the appearance of this work in tombs seems to be derived from its containing a section on the theology of the *ba*, and the links between the king and the sun god

The inner part of the burial chamber comprised a sunken crypt with a high, vaulted ceiling (fig. 99). The crypt had been a feature of royal tombs since the time of Amenhotep II, but hitherto the ceiling above it had been a flat continuation of that of the pillared section of the burial chamber. Now, its curved surface hosted a vast astronomical ceiling, in yellow on blue, of the ancient Egyptians' classical conception of the sky, going back at least to the Twelfth Dynasty. Sethy's version represents an advance over the previous New Kingdom version, in the tomb of Senenmut (TT353), in containing all five visible planets.

FIGURE 97 The entrance walls of chamber Ja, showing parts of the Third and Fourth Hours of the Book of Gates; pillar-face Ab of chamber J, with the king before Horus, can be seen through the doorway.

FIGURE 98 The central tableau of the Book of the Divine Cow on the rear wall of chamber Je.

FIGURE 99 The crypt of chamber J. Visible on the walls are the Second and Third Hours of the Book of *Amduat*: at the top-left corner of the upper register of the *Amduat* text is the niche for the southern of the four magic bricks that protected each of the cardinal points. The astronomical ceiling shows, on the southern section of ceiling (left), the decans (small constellations used in ancient Egyptian astronomy) of the heliacal rising stars for each of the ten-day weeks of the Egyptian civil calendar, plus the five epagomenal days. Underneath these decans (center left) are representations of Sirius and Orion, and all the visible planets. On the north section of ceiling (right) are the lunar protective gods, each with a lunar disk on their head as they face a representation of the so-called Northern Constellations.

FIGURE 100 The south wall of the crypt of chamber J, with the First Hour of the *Amduat*. As in fig. 86, there is a rectangle of experimental cleaning; to the right and left of this are further magic brick-niches, the latter being for the eastern brick, which would have been problematic to accommodate among the pillars on that side. At the bottom left is the doorway to chamber Jb. The small niche on the right, containing an image of Osiris with the Opening of the Mouth performed by Anubis, differs from the rest of the chamber in being decorated in flat paint, rather than raised relief.

The right-hand wall of the crypt was occupied by the Third Hour of the *Amduat*, continuing a sequence begun on the opposite wall, which bore the First Hour (fig. 100), with the Second Hour on the rear wall. A subsidiary room opened from each wall of the crypt, those at the right (Jd, fig. 101) and rear (Jc) being undecorated, although the latter was of considerable size and had a ceiling supported by four pillars. The room on the left side (Jb) was also pillared, but was in this case extensively decorated, with the

FIGURE 101 The doorway through into chamber Jd, shown here while used as a store for fragments awaiting restoration to the walls.

Sixth, Seventh, and Eighth Hours of the *Amduat*, and also featured an unusual bench—presumably to support funerary equipment—around three walls (fig. 102). The pillars had in most cases a single image on each of their faces of either a deity or the deified king (fig. 124), the exceptions being the outermost faces, on which the king

embraced aspects of Osiris. Unlike the other subsidiary rooms of the burial chamber, this one had been sealed after the burial.[22]

From the floor of the crypt, a further set of galleries, once concealed by overpaving, dived steeply into the rock.[23] The first part (K1–7) was cut though the *tafl* layer directly under the limestone of the main part of the tomb, and comprised seven sections, divided by a series of rock-cut gates, with the floors of the most steeply sloped elements comprising stairways, incorporating a ramp down the center. Though found in the Royal Tomb at Amarna, and previously in pyramids of the later Middle Kingdom, this feature had not been used inside a Valley of the Kings tomb before. The quality of the rock made work difficult, and many features are now difficult to distinguish.

However, at a depth of some sixty meters below the floor of the burial chamber crypt, a new stratum of chalk allowed the far easier cutting of the remaining three galleries (K8–10), also distinguished from the upper ones by the two stairways (K8 and K10) in lacking a central ramp. The slightly sloping K9 displayed the beginning of preparations for decoration. But the final stairway was never finished, the galleries terminating abruptly in a last unfinished step 92.14

FIGURE 102 Chamber Jb, called by Belzoni the "Sideboard Room," on account of the shelves presumably intended to support funerary equipment. The walls bear the Sixth to Eighth Hours of the *Amduat*.

meters below the floor of the crypt and far below tomb KV42 (ultimately owned by Meryetre, wife of Thutmose III) on the other side of the Valley from KV17 (fig. 78).

These lower galleries, with a linear extent of 174 meters, to be added to the ninety meters of the upper tomb, make KV17 by far the longest tomb in the Valley of the Kings. Their purpose, however, remains obscure. One option is that the king's body was to lie at the end, in a never-cut final chamber (see further just below). Others have suggested that the plan had been to place the king's mummy much deeper underground than the conventional burial chamber, an objective frustrated by the king's premature death. It has also been theorized that the tunnel might have been intended to reach the water table, which is certainly not far below the point where cutting was stopped, mirroring the water element of the Osireion at Abydos.[24]

Whatever may have been aspired to, the actual burial of the king is certain to have been carried out in the crypt. The installation was, however, innovative in that, in contrast to what had been provided for all kings since at least Hatshepsut (including Rameses I, fig. 12),[25] no hardstone sarcophagus was included in Sethy I's burial outfit.[26] Furthermore, rather than the solely wood/gold set of coffins provided for earlier kings,[27] Sethy was given a calcite outer coffin of a wholly novel design (fig. 103).[28]

FIGURE 103 Sethy I's calcite coffin trough (Soane M470).

As to why the hardstone sarcophagus, a feature of kings' burials since the Fourth Dynasty, was omitted is unclear, but it could be linked with the enigmatic lower galleries of the tomb. If it had indeed been intended to place the royal mummy at the end, it would have been all but impossible to introduce a traditional hardstone sarcophagus down the steeply sloping (and in their upper section, geologically only marginally stable) lower galleries. In contrast, a relatively light and compact calcite coffin could certainly have been taken down to a small chamber that could have been regarded as the equivalent of a sarcophagus.[29]

Whether or not intended, such an installation was not carried out, but it is highly unlikely that the calcite coffin was left without any sarcophagus-equivalent enclosure. The sarcophagus of Tutankhamun had been surrounded by four shrines and a frame-mounted pall, while a papyrus plan of the tomb of Rameses IV (KV2) shows that a similar scheme was still current during the Twentieth Dynasty. It would thus seem certain that the actual burial of Sethy I also included such shrines. Given that a sarcophagus was interposed between the inner shrine and the outer anthropoid coffin in the cases of both Tutankhamun and Rameses IV, and that a sarcophagus was present in such intact private burials as those of Maihirpri (KV36), Yuya and Tjuiu (KV46), and Sennedjem (TT1),[30]

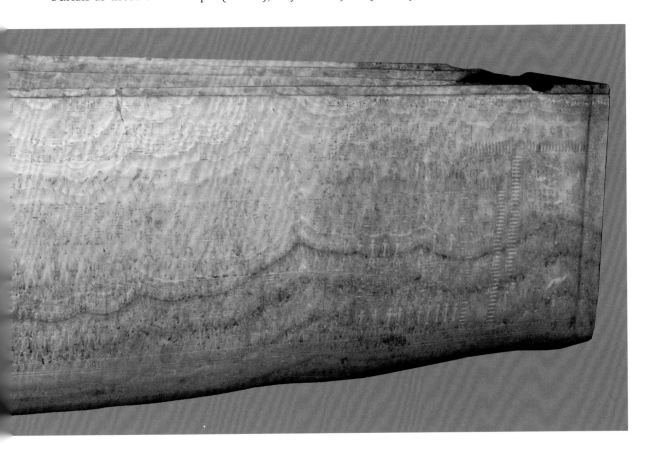

it seems highly probable that one was provided for Sethy—but that like the private examples, it was made of wood.

As far as the potential decoration of such a piece is concerned, one option is a continuation of the Eighteenth Dynasty pattern, ultimately deriving from Middle Kingdom practice, of a simple arrangement of figures of Isis and Nephthys at the head and foot, with the Four Sons of Horus and forms of Anubis (and perhaps Thoth) on the long sides, with appropriate texts.[31] This was the pattern employed on the sarcophagus of Rameses I, but when stone royal sarcophagi reappeared under Merenptah, decoration had shifted fundamentally, with schemes based upon the Books of *Amduat* and *Gates*, and other underworld-based elements.

That this may have been the approach taken on the putative wooden sarcophagus of Sethy I may be suggested by the switch seen on the sarcophagus of Sethy's private contemporary Sennedjem (and also on that of his son, Khonsu). Here, the Eighteenth Dynasty pattern was replaced by extensive texts from the Book of the Dead and a much more eclectic set of vignettes, although still including the protective deities. On the other hand, the older scheme continued to be found on the troughs of private coffins beyond the time of Sethy I and, as will shortly be described, the Book of Gates appeared on the calcite coffin, perhaps pointing to a more traditional sarcophagus scheme. Unfortunately, as no trace of the putative sarcophagus has ever come to light, the question must remain moot.

While of the anthropoid form generally used for coffins since the Second Intermediate Period, Sethy's calcite coffin did not employ the *rishi* (feathered) scheme used on all surviving earlier New Kingdom royal coffins, most spectacularly on those of Tutankhamun. Rather, the walls of the trough, both inside and out, and parts of the exterior of the lid were adorned with the Book of Gates. No earlier examples of such decoration on a coffin are known, although this was employed on later royal calcite coffins (cf. below), and also on a fragmentary granite example, usurped by the Twenty-first Dynasty high priest of Amun, Menkheperre, and found at Abydos.[32] The original owner may have been a son of Rameses II—perhaps Meryamun or Merymaat.

On Sethy's calcite coffin, the First Hour occupied the exterior of the foot of the trough, the Second through Fifth Hours proceeding clockwise around the trough and then up to the margins of the lid, which bore the Sixth, Seventh, and Eighth Hours, again clockwise from the foot (fig. 104). The sequence continued within the trough, running from the Ninth Hour on the left-proper side of the head around to the concluding tableau at the top of the head (fig. 105). The floor of the trough was occupied by a full-length figure of the goddess Nut, a common image on the floors—and interior of the lids—of coffins and sarcophagi, and commonly invoked on the exterior of the lid. In

Sethy's case, the goddess's image was surrounded by texts from the Book of the Dead, as was much of the inside of the lid, although the loss of so much of the central and foot portion of the latter makes it difficult to produce a comprehensive reconstruction. On the other hand, remains survive of a winged sun disk embracing the top of the king's head, recumbent jackals at his shoulders, and a winged being over his chest.

FIGURE 104 The decoration of the exterior of Sethy I's calcite coffin, including a partial reconstruction of the lid.

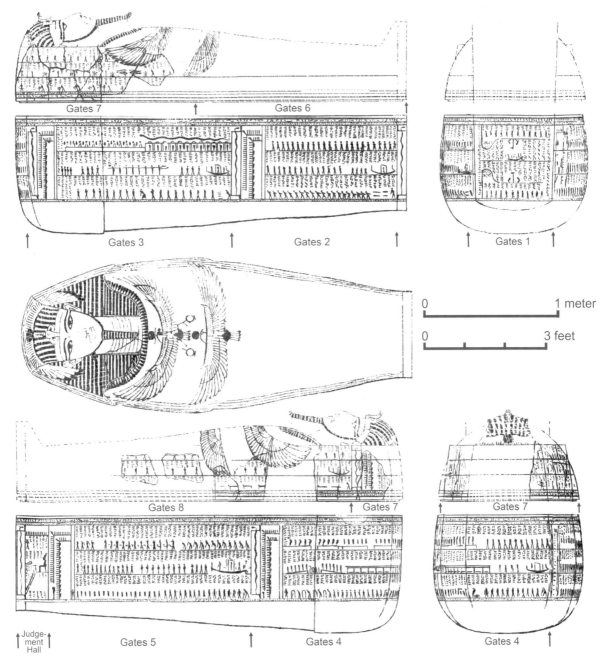

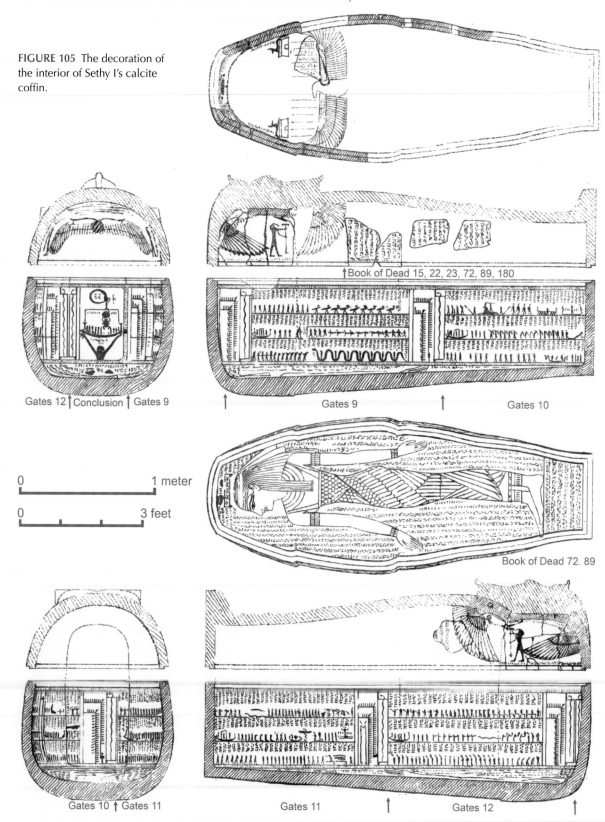

FIGURE 105 The decoration of the interior of Sethy I's calcite coffin.

Book of Dead 15, 22, 23, 72, 89, 180

Gates 12 ↑ Conclusion ↑ Gates 9

Gates 9

Gates 10

0   1 meter

0   3 feet

Book of Dead 72. 89

Gates 10 ↑ Gates 11

Gates 11

Gates 12

The destruction of so much of the lid also presents problems with assessing the decoration of much of its exterior. However, while the face is entirely lost, it is clear that the king was shown wearing the *nemes* headdress and that the areas below the collar and across the lower torso were spanned by vulture-winged beings (fig. 106).

As to what originally lay inside the calcite coffin, earlier royal and private practice was for there to be a maximum of three nested anthropoid coffins, suggesting two within. On the parallel of Tutankhamun, this could have been a solid gold inner example, with a gilded wooden middle coffin, although later in the New Kingdom, Sethnakhte had a cartonnage inner container, and Rameses III had

FIGURE 106 Fragment, probably from the lid of the calcite coffin of Sethy I. However, as no royal name survives, it is possible that it comes from the coffin of a later king of the dynasty (BM EA29948).

one carved out of a log of cedar wood.[33] If indeed of gold, Sethy's inner coffin will have been melted down in antiquity, but, as described in Chapter 4, the king's mummy was ultimately found in a heavily modified wooden coffin that, from its size and remains of original features, had clearly been manufactured to be the middle example from a royal coffin nest (fig. 109) and would certainly have fit within Sethy's calcite coffin. While it is known that a number of kings ended up in coffins that were not their original ones during the renewals and removals that took place from the end of the New Kingdom until the beginning of the Twenty-second Dynasty, at least some (such as Thutmose III) kept their own.

Perhaps the second most important element of a burial, after the mummy and its sheltering coffins and sarcophagi, was the canopic equipment, containing the viscera removed during the embalming process. Under Amenhotep II, a distinctive form of canopic chest had been developed for kingly use, carved from a single block of calcite, with four cavities bored out to take the place of conventional separate canopic jars, which had been used down to the reign of Thutmose III.[34] Each of these was stopped with a lid in the form of the king's head, and, to judge from Tutankhamun's installation, the visceral bundles within each cavity may have been enclosed in miniature coffins of gold. High status private examples (Tjuiu in KV46) suggest that an alternative may have been to adorn the bundles with a gilded cartonnage mask.

Externally, these calcite chests had their corners enfolded by the four protective goddesses, Isis, Nephthys, Neith, and Selqet, which acquired wings under Horemheb. From the tomb of Sethy I came a single fragment of just such a chest (fig. 107). Its principal visible difference from the corresponding part of that of Horemheb is that a hand protrudes from under one of the wings. This shows that, unlike the chests of Horemheb (and Tutankhamun), but like the earlier example of Amenhotep II and various ones belonging to private individuals, two of its faces were also adorned with pairs of the Four Sons of Horus. It is unclear whether the depiction of these genii continued under Rameses II, as the one fragment of his chest does not include the appropriate area; this does, however, show that under Rameses the simply-molded details of the goddesses were replaced by a new technique including glass inlays.

The sheer volume and variety of material that might be buried with a New Kingdom king is indicated by the tomb of Tutankhamun, but, like all other royal tombs in the Valley of the Kings, that of Sethy I had been comprehensively robbed and stripped of its contents in antiquity. When it was entered in 1817, all that apparently remained were a large number of *shabti* figures of wood and faience, principally in chamber Jc, some wooden figures around 1.3 meters high with circular cavities inside, presumably for papyri, found "on each side" of two of the smaller annexes to the burial chamber,

plus the remains of other figures of wood and faience. In addition, a mummified bovid was found in chamber Jc (see page 113).

Estimates of the number of known *shabti*s of Sethy I vary between some four hundred and as high as seven hundred: examples are spread through dozens of collections around the world. It is assumed that they all ultimately came from KV17,[35] although it is known that *shabti*s could be used in votive deposits as well as in tombs.[36] Sethy's *shabti*s fell into four principal kinds (fig. 108).[37] First, there was a small group (perhaps no more than ten) of large faience examples,

FIGURE 107 Left: the only known fragment of the canopic chest of Sethy I (Soane X74); right: the reconstructed canopic chest of Horemheb, which closely resembled that of Sethy. The main difference between the two chests was that Sethy's included representations of the Four Sons of Horus; from KV57 (Cairo TR 9/12/22/1–14).

FIGURE 108 Examples of principal *shabti* types from the tomb of Sethy I (a. MMA 26.7.919; b. BM EA8897; c. BM EA33919; d. BM EA8900; e. Munich ÄS443; f. BM EA37579).

up to thirty centimeters high, wearing the *nemes* headdress (some with a uraeus, some without), with the full version of the Book of the Dead chapter 6 *shabti* spell (BD6). Second, there were smaller faience pieces, around half the size of the previous type, each with a tripartite headdress and a shorter version of the *shabti* spell. Third, and representing the largest proportion of Sethy's *shabtis*, were wooden (in at least some cases juniper) figures around twenty centimeters tall inscribed with the shorter BD6 and originally covered with black

a   b   c   d   e   f

resin. Fourth were examples in a crystalline calcite, around the same size as the smaller faience pieces and also wearing tripartite headdresses, but with brief inscriptions simply invoking "the Osiris Menmaatre." There are also a small number in green-glazed steatite.

Curiously, although wooden figures from the tomb of Rameses I are now in the British Museum, none from that of Sethy I can now be identified there, nor do any seem to have found their way into other collections. While none of the Rameses I pieces have spaces for papyri within them, they include many of the types that one would have expected originally to have been in Sethy's tomb: figures of denizens of the underworld and a pair of guardian statues, all originally covered with black resin.[38] Many of these have close parallels among material recovered from the tombs of Horemheb and Tutankhamun (with the exception that the latter were generally covered with gold foil, rather than resin). The bovid found in chamber Jc, dubbed by the original excavator that of an Apis bull (the sacred animal of Ptah) (see page 127), was presumably actually a victual mummy, of a kind common in New Kingdom tombs.[39]

4 LIMBO

Sadly, Sethy was not fated to rest undisturbed in his sumptuous sepulcher. Within a century of his death, the country was convulsed by a civil war between the king's great-great-grandson, Sethy II, and a usurper, Amenmeses, apparently the second Sethy's own younger son.[1] In the aftermath, a child king, Siptah, reigned for five years under the direction of Bay, an official of Syrian heritage, and Sethy II's widow, Tawosret, until the 'Syrian' was executed; a year later Siptah was dead and Tawosret had become female pharaoh. A further civil war then took place until a certain Sethnakhte was victorious, founding the Twentieth Dynasty. His successor, Rameses III, successfully defended Egypt against external enemies, before economic and political crises culminated in his assassination.[2] His successors, all named Rameses (IV–XI), then presided over a steadily declining situation, with Egyptian control of Nubia crumbling and banditry from the West disrupting life even in Thebes, where corruption was seemingly now endemic. Tomb robbery took hold, and even the royal cemeteries became the victims of plunderers during the reign of Rameses IX.[3]

Civil conflicts also arose, and in their wake a new era of 'Renaissance' (*wḥm-mswt*, cf. page 18) was proclaimed within the reign of Rameses XI. It is in Year 6 of this that we hear of the fate of the burial of Sethy I: on II *3ḫt* 7 a docket was written on the lid of the wooden coffin that now contained his mummy (fig. 109). Probably originally the

FIGURE 109 The wooden coffin that housed the mummy of Sethy I from at least the beginning of the eleventh century. It was certainly originally made for a king but had been heavily restored after the removal of its original gilded and inlaid decoration, of which only the glass and stone eyes remained. The face had been recarved, leaving the eyes greatly oversized, with only the lappets preserving traces of the original royal nemes headdress. The lost uraeus on the brow was drawn in ink on the replastered and whitewashed surface (Cairo CG61019).

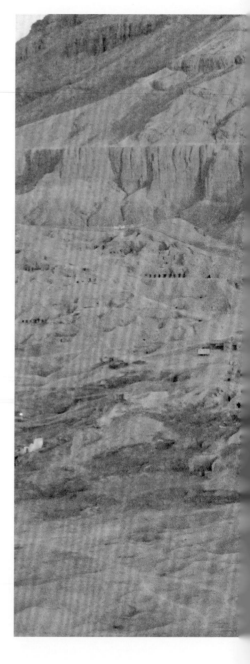

king's gilded and inlaid middle coffin (page 110), it was now almost unrecognizable as such, long since despoiled of its gold foil and glass inlay, with its ruined surfaces tidied up, replastered, and whitewashed.

The docket read: "The day the vizier, general and high priest of Amun-Re-King-of-the-Gods Herihor proceeded to repeat the burial of King Menmaatre, LPH, Son of Re Sethy-Merenptah [LPH], by the Agent Hirenamunpena and the Trainee Prepayuyotef."[4] This "repeating of the burial" had clearly included the restoration of the coffin, and also the rewrapping of the mummy it housed. The latter had been stripped of its original bandages by robbers, whose violence in their search for jewelry—then or later (see the following paragraph)—ultimately caused the head to break off, and much of the abdomen to be broken away (fig. 126).

Presumably restored in some workshop away from the king's tomb, probably at Medinet Habu, by then the headquarters of the Theban necropolis,[5] the coffined body was then returned to KV17. Some years later it was joined by the likewise restored (and re-coffined) mummy of Sethy's son, Rameses II. This had initially been restored around the same time as Sethy I's mummy, a docket recording a "repeating of burial" on III *prt* 15 of Year 6 of the *whm-mswt*—presumably again in his own tomb (KV7). However, a further docket (on Rameses's mummy shroud) of Year 15 (of the reign of Nesibanebdjed I—some two decades after Year 6 of the *whm-mswt*) notes that on III *3ht* 6 the high priest of Amun Panedjem I "renewed" Rameses and buried him "in the tomb of the Osiris King Menmaatre, LPH."[6] Clearly, a further raid had been made in the interim on Rameses II's tomb, and, having restored the mummy once more, it had been decided that Sethy's tomb might be a safer refuge.

However, a further attack on KV17 is indicated by a bandage docket found on Sethy's mummy, six layers below the outermost layer of wrappings. This recorded Year 7, II *prt* 10, as a "day of the burial of King Menmaatre, LPH."[7] That this unattributed date belonged to the reign of Pasebkhanut I, successor of Nesibanebdjed I, is indicated by another bandage on the mummy that was manufactured in Year 6 during the pontificate of Menkheperre,[8] which ran essentially in parallel with the reign of Pasebkhanut I (his brother).[9]

TT320

At some point, the mummy of Rameses I was moved into KV17 from the next-door KV16 to join his son and grandson. It was certainly there on IV *prt* 17 of Year 10 of King Siamun (some nine decades after the move of Rameses II to his father's tomb and seven since the last record of restoring Sethy I's mummy). On that day, as recorded by dockets added to all three kings' coffins, Rameses I, Sethy I, and Rameses II were "brought out from the tomb of King Menmaatre

FIGURE 110 The location of TT320, south of Deir el-Bahari, where the mummy of Sethy I lay, along with those of many of his peers, for nearly three millennia following its placement there during the later tenth century. It seems likely that the tomb was originally that of the Eighteenth Dynasty queen Ahmes-Nefertiry, wife of Ahmose I.

Sethy-Merenptah, in order to cause [them] to enter into the cliff-tomb of Inhapi, which is an important place . . . in which Amenhotep rests."[10] Three days later (on Day 20), the mummies arrived at their destination, another docket being added to their coffins to that effect.[11] A pair of cartouches were probably added to the breast of Sethy's coffin at that time, partly obscuring the old *whm-mswt*-era docket.

The location of the tomb of Inhapi has never been identified, but as she was a wife of King Taa of the late Seventeenth Dynasty, it almost certainly lay at Dra Abu'l-Naga, between the Valley of the Kings and Sethy's memorial temple at Qurna, where lay all known royal tombs of that dynasty. This idea is reinforced by the fact that the 'Amenhotep' named as already lodging in the tomb was Amenhotep I, second king of the Eighteenth Dynasty, who also appears to have had his tomb at Dra Abu'l-Naga (see page 70).[12]

No records survive to document the next move (or even moves) of the mummies that now lay in the tomb of Inhapi, nor whether they were joined there by further displaced royal bodies. Nevertheless, it is clear that the Valley of the Kings was being cleared of its kingly occupants, the only ones left behind being a group successfully hidden in the tomb of Amenhotep II (KV35), plus any whose tombs were by then wholly lost—in particular that of Tutankhamun. Ultimately, those removed from the Valley were placed, together with bodies from other locations, in a tomb just south of Deir el-Bahari (TT320, fig. 110). This seems to have originally belonged to Queen Ahmes-Neferity of the early Eighteenth Dynasty,[13] and was much later taken over for the Twenty-first Dynasty high priest of Amun Panedjem II (buried there on the same day that Sethy I and the two Rameses were moved into the tomb of Inhapi) and his family. It was some time after the burial of the last of the latter, which probably took place during the second decade of the reign of Shoshenq I (around half a century after Sethy had been moved to the tomb of Inhapi),[14] that some thirty royal mummies were placed in the tomb.[15] Among them was Sethy I, whose mummy was apparently one of the very last to be placed in the tomb, being found only a short way from the tomb entrance with only three coffins in front of it. There Sethy would sleep undisturbed with his fellows for the next twenty-eight centuries.

5 Resurrection

Remembrance

The end of paganism and use of the hieroglyphic script at the end of the fourth century AD meant that any records surviving from Sethy's time henceforth became unreadable, and any residual memory of his reign depended on writings in other languages. The work of the third century BC writer Manetho, which provided a residual chronicle of the ancient kings of Egypt, itself only preserved in the books of later excerptors, is badly confused for the end of the Eighteenth and the whole of the Nineteenth Dynasty. Thus, although a "Sethos"—apparently a Greek rendering of "Sethy"—features in the latter, he is misplaced and given a reign length five times that of Sethy I (presumably his prototype) in all extant versions.[1]

The name "Sethos" had also appeared in the fifth-century work of Herodotus, but it was applied there to a wholly different king, contemporary with Sennacherib of Assyria (705–681 BC)—the Twenty-fifth Dynasty monarch Shabaka.[2] As a result, the name "Sethos" survived in Western consciousness, even if divorced from its true prototype, and became well known via a novel by Jean Terrasson (1670–1750), *Sethos: histoire ou vie tirée des monumens anecdotes de l'ancienne Egypte*, first published in Paris in 1731. Translated into English the following year as *The Life of Sethos: taken from private memoirs of the ancient Egyptians*, into Italian in 1734, and into German in 1777, the novel's literary conceit was that it was based on a real second century AD manuscript. This misled many into taking it for a genuine source for ancient Egyptian culture, including playing an important role in the development of freemasonry—and thus becoming an inspiration for Mozart's opera *The Magic Flute* (1791).[3]

Rome

On the other hand, while the real Sethy had long been lost as a historical figure, a monument of the king—albeit unrecognized as such—had made a reappearance in the middle of the fifteenth century. Following Augustus's conquest of Egypt in 30 BC, one of the obelisks erected by Sethy I at Heliopolis (see page 29) had been removed to Rome and re-erected on the spina (central barrier) of the Circus Maximus in Rome in 10 BC (fig. 111). It served as a monument to the emperor's victory in Egypt and

FIGURE 111 Rome's Circus Maximus, where one of Sethy I's Heliopolitan obelisks stood for some five hundred years.

inaugurated a long fashion for the appropriation of obelisks from Egypt to Rome.[4] Its texts were at some point translated into Greek by a certain Hermapion and published by Ammianus Marcellinus in the late fourth century AD.[5]

That the obelisk soon became an admired monument is indicated by the fact that a reduced copy was eventually made of it, albeit with hieroglyphs and other decorative elements sadly debased as compared with the original (fig. 112).[6] Who commissioned the copy is unknown, but the stratigraphy of its base, in the Gardens of Sallust, suggests a third century AD date for its erection, although some have suggested a connection with the Egyptophilia of Emperor Hadrian (76–138).

The 'real' Sethy I obelisk was later joined in the Circus by another, brought by Constantine I (312–337) from Karnak (where it had been erected by Thutmose IV) and re-erected in Rome in 357 by Constantius II (337–361). This obelisk was later purposely overturned, leaving the Sethy obelisk standing. The latter also later fell, perhaps during the fifth century, its broken pieces soon becoming buried among the debris in the Circus. It was rediscovered by Leone Battista Alberti (1404–72) in 1471 but was then lost sight of until 1586, when the existence of the two Circus obelisks was brought to the attention of Pope Sixtus V (r. 1585–90), who was particularly interested in such monuments. He had already had the architect Domenico Fontana (1543–1607) move the one then-standing obelisk in Rome, outside St. Peter's Basilica, to a new, more prominent site, and had begun work to re-erect an obelisk that had once stood at the Mausoleum of Augustus. Now, Fontana was ordered to rediscover the Circus pair and re-erect them as well. The ex-Karnak obelisk was found in February 1587 and was placed outside the church of San Giovanni in Laterano the following summer.

The Sethy obelisk was uncovered by Matteo da Castello (1555–1632) four days after the other; its fragments were dug up and then stored in the Via dei Carceri, pending a decision about where it should be placed. On 18 July, the obelisk was formally presented to the people of Rome by the pope and erected in the Piazza del Popolo, the last of the broken pieces being fixed in place on 3 March 1588. A cross was added to the tip, to mark its transition from a pagan to a Christian monument, on the 29th. It has stood in the piazza ever since, being cleaned and restored in 2005 (figs. 113 & 114).

Sixtus V had also planned to re-erect the Roman copy of the Sethy obelisk, but it was not until the eighteenth century that plans finally came

FIGURE 112 The Roman copy of Sethy I's obelisk, now on the Spanish Steps in Rome. While the hieroglyphs are fairly well rendered, the tableau of the king before Re-Horakhty at the bottom is wholly un-Egyptian in its style.

FIGURE 113 Sethy I's Heliopolitan obelisk, in the Piazza del Popolo, Rome, where it has stood since 1589.

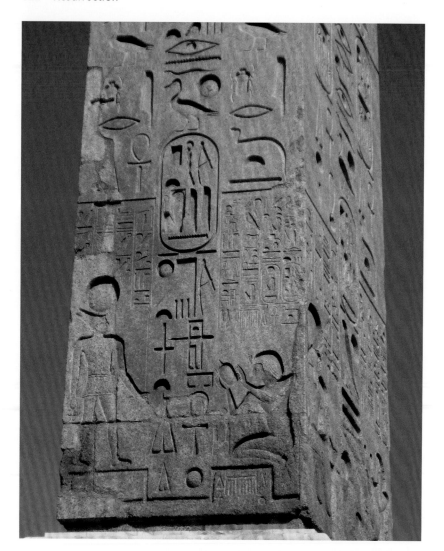

FIGURE 114 Base of the obelisk, showing sixteenth-century restorations.

to fruition, one abortive project envisaging its translation to outside Notre Dame in Paris. Finally, in 1786, it was proposed that it should be placed outside the church of Trinita dei Monti, at the top of Rome's Spanish Steps. Re-erection in that place was finally achieved in April 1789.

During the centuries when these and other re-erected obelisks were exposed in Rome, they were key exhibits in many of the speculations as to how hieroglyphs might be read. However, most regarded the obelisks' texts as containing deeply philosophical concepts, and as a result doubted the validity of Hermapion's quite accurate translation of the text on the Sethy I obelisk.[7] However, only a decade after its Roman copy had been finally placed upright once again, the key to understanding hieroglyphs had been found, and the events that would lead to the rediscovery of ancient Egypt in general— and Sethy I in particular—put in train.

'Belzoni's Tomb'

The ultimately abortive French invasion of Egypt in 1798 was not merely a military enterprise but also a scientific one, and a combination of the two resulted in the discovery in July 1799, during the renovation of a fort at Rashid (Rosetta), of a fragment of trilingual stela—the Rosetta Stone—that would prove the key to the eventual decipherment of the ancient Egyptian language. The expedition sparked a new interest in the land and its history, while the appointment of Muhammad 'Ali (1769–1849) as governor of Egypt (since 1517 an Ottoman province) changed the whole complexion of the country. The publication of its scientific results, the *Description de l'Égypte*, included plans and elevations of Sethy's Qurna temple (dubbed a "palais"), and also of the outer hypostyle halls and seven shrines of the Abydene temple, although the rest of the complex remained deeply buried.

Muhammad 'Ali wished to modernize Egypt, and as a result many Europeans traveled there with a view to making their fortunes. Among them was Giovanni Battista Belzoni (1778–1823, fig. 115), who arrived in 1815 following a varied career, including most famously as a circus performer, to put forward a hydraulic machine of his own invention.[8] His demonstration of this in the spring of 1816 proved unsuccessful, but Belzoni was then engaged by the recently arrived British consul general Henry Salt (1780–1827)[9] to remove a colossal bust of Rameses II from the king's memorial temple, the Ramesseum, at Thebes, successfully bringing it down to the Nile bank in August 1816.

Salt, like many of his fellow diplomats, was engaged in putting together a collection of Egyptian antiquities for ultimate sale (although Salt had a genuine interest in archaeology as well), and for the next few years he employed Belzoni as his principal agent. Belzoni also undertook work on his own behalf, the dividing line between this work and that undertaken under the auspices of Salt being, on occasion, rather fuzzy.

FIGURE 115 Giovanni Belzoni.

In the autumn of 1816, Belzoni successfully opened the tomb of Ay (WV23) in the Western Valley of the Kings, and a year later returned to the same area, finding an unfinished late Eighteenth Dynasty royal tomb, WV25 (probably intended for Akhenaten when Amenhotep IV), containing a Third Intermediate Period or later cache of mummies.[10] In October 1817, he moved to the main part of the Valley, finding first the Twentieth Dynasty tomb of Prince Montjuhirkopeshef (KV19), and then the small Eighteenth Dynasty tomb, KV21. Soon afterward, the tomb of Rameses I was brought to light, and then, after a few days' break:

> On the 16th [of October] I recommenced my excavations in the valley of Beban el Malook, and pointed out the fortunate spot, which has paid me for all the trouble I took in my researches. I may call this a fortunate day, one of the best perhaps of my life; I do not mean to say, that fortune has made me rich, for I do not consider all rich men fortunate; but she has given me that satisfaction, that extreme pleasure, which wealth cannot purchase; the pleasure of discovering what has been long sought in vain, and of presenting the world with a new and perfect monument of Egyptian antiquity, which can be recorded as superior to any other in point of grandeur, style and preservation, appearing as if just finished on the day we entered it; and what I found in it will show its great superiority to all others. Not fifteen yards from the last tomb I described [that of Rameses I], I caused the earth to be opened at the foot of a steep hill, and under a torrent, which, when it rains, pours a great quantity of water over the very spot I have caused to be dug. No one could imagine, that the ancient Egyptians would make the entrance into such an immense and superb excavation just under a torrent of water; but I had strong reasons to suppose, that there was a tomb in that place, from indications I had observed in my pursuit. The Fellahs who were accustomed to dig were all of opinion, that there was nothing in that spot, as the situation of this tomb differed from that of any other. I continued the work however, and the next day, the 17th, in the evening, we perceived the part of the rock that was cut, and formed the entrance. On the 18th, early in the morning, the task was resumed, and about noon the workmen reached the entrance, which was eighteen feet below the surface of the ground. The appearance indicated, that the tomb was of the first rate: but still I did not expect to find such a one as it really proved to be. The Fellahs advanced till they saw that it was probably a large tomb, when they protested they could go no farther, the tomb was so much choked up with large stones, which they could not get out of the passage. I descended, examined the place, pointed out to them where they might dig, and in an hour there was room enough for me to enter through a passage that the earth had left under the ceiling of the first corridor, which is thirty-six feet two inches long; and eight feet eight inches wide, and, when cleared of the ruins, six feet nine inches high. I perceived immediately by the painting on the ceiling, and by the hieroglyphics in basso relievo, which were to be seen where the earth did not reach, that this was the entrance into a large and magnificent tomb . . . [fig. 116].

FIGURE 116 The entrance to the tomb of Sethy I as it was in
1817/18; the decoration of the lintel is now entirely destroyed.

The more I saw, the more I was eager to see, such being the nature of man: but I was checked in my anxiety at this time, for at the end of [the first set of corridors] I reached a large pit, which intercepted my progress . . . . On the opposite side of the pit facing the entrance I perceived a small aperture two feet wide and two feet six inches high, and at the bottom of the wall a quantity of rubbish. A rope fastened to a piece of wood, that was laid across the passage against the projections which form a kind of door, appears to have been used by the ancients for descending into the pit; and from the small aperture on the opposite side hung another, which reached the bottom, no doubt for the purpose of ascending. We could clearly perceive, that the water which entered the passages from the torrents crumbled to dust on touching them. At the bottom of the pit were several pieces of wood, placed against the side of it, so as to assist the person who was to ascend by the rope into the aperture. I saw the impossibility of proceeding at the moment, [but t]he next day, the 19th, by means of a long beam we succeeded in sending a man up into the aperture, and having contrived to make a bridge of two beams, we crossed the pit. The little aperture we found to be an opening forced through a wall, that had entirely closed the entrance, which was as large as the corridor. The Egyptians had closely shut it up, plastered the wall over, and painted it like the rest of the sides of the pit, so that but for the aperture, it would have been impossible to suppose, that there was any; farther proceeding; and any one would conclude, that the tomb ended with the pit. The rope in the inside of the wall did not fall to dust, but remained pretty strong, the water not having reached it at all; and the wood to which it was attached was in good preservation. It was owing to this method of keeping the damp out of the inner parts of the tomb that they are so well preserved.[11]

Belzoni's last remark would tragically be shown to be all too correct the following year.

When we had passed through the little aperture, we found ourselves in a beautiful hall . . . in which were four pillars . . . . At the end of this room, which I call the entrance-hall, and opposite the aperture, is a large door, from which three steps lead down into a chamber with two pillars . . . . I gave it the name of the drawing-room; for it is covered with figures, which, though only outlined, are so fine and perfect, that you would think they had been drawn only the day before. Returning into the entrance-hall, we saw on the left of the aperture a large staircase, which descended into a corridor . . . . We perceived, that the paintings became more perfect as we advanced farther into the interior. They retained their gloss, or a kind of varnish over the colours, which had a beautiful effect. The figures are painted on a white ground. At the end of this corridor we descended ten steps . . . into another . . . . From this we entered a small chamber . . . , to which I gave the name of the Room of Beauties; for it is adorned with the most beautiful figures in basso relievo, like all the rest, and painted. When standing in the centre of this chamber, the traveller is surrounded by an assembly of Egyptian gods and goddesses. Proceeding farther, we entered a large hall

[with] two rows of square pillars, three on each side of the entrance, forming a line with the corridors . . . . This hall I termed the Hall of Pillars . . . . At the end of this hall we entered a large saloon, with an arched roof or ceiling . . . . At the same end of the room, and facing the Hall of Pillars, we entered by a large door into another chamber with four pillars, one of which is fallen down . . . . I named it the Bull's, or Apis' Room, as we found the carcass of a bull in it, embalmed with asphaltum; and also, scattered in various places, an immense quantity of small wooden figures of mummies six or eight inches long, and covered with asphaltum to preserve them. There were some other figures of fine earth baked, coloured blue, and strongly varnished. On each side of the two little rooms were some wooden statues standing erect, four feet high, with a circular hollow inside, as if to contain a roll of papyrus, which I have no doubt they did. We found likewise fragments of other statues of wood and of composition.

But the description of what we found in the centre of the saloon, and which I have reserved till this place, merits the most particular attention, not having its equal in the world, and being such as we had no idea could exist. It is a sarcophagus of the finest oriental alabaster . . . and it is transparent, when a light is placed in the inside of it. It is minutely sculptured within and without with several hundred figures, which do not exceed two inches in height . . . . I cannot give an adequate idea of this beautiful and invaluable piece of antiquity, and can only say, that nothing has been brought into Europe from Egypt that can be compared with it. The cover was not there: it had been taken out, and broken into several pieces, which we found in digging before the first entrance. The sarcophagus was over a staircase in the centre of the saloon, which communicated with a subterraneous passage, leading downwards, three hundred feet in length. At the end of this passage we found a great quantity of bats' dung, which choked it up, so that we could go no farther without digging. It was nearly filled up too by the falling in of the upper part. One hundred feet from the entrance is a staircase in good preservation; but the rock below changes its substance, from a beautiful solid calcareous stone, becoming a kind of black rotten slate, which crumbles into dust only by touching . . . . Some large blocks of stone were placed under the sarcophagus horizontally, level with the pavement of the saloon, that no one might perceive any stairs or subterranean passage was there.[12]

The news of the discovery soon spread, Hamed Aga, the governor of Qena, arriving expecting to find a rumored golden cockerel filled with diamonds and pearls. Salt, accompanying Somerset Lowry-Corry, 2nd Earl of Belmore (1774–1841),[13] and his entourage on a tour of Egypt visited on 16 November with the French consul general, Bernardino Drovetti (1776–1852)[14]—a long-term antagonist of Salt and Belzoni— viewing the tomb on the 20th.

Belzoni then returned to Cairo, but Salt remained behind, making drawings in the tomb and also spending four months excavating in the Valley himself, including apparently clearing the outer galleries of the tomb of Rameses II (KV7) and recovering a guardian statue from that of Rameses IX (KV6). Preparatory work also seems to have been undertaken toward removing not only Sethy's calcite coffin but also the coffer of the sarcophagus of Rameses III in KV11 from the Valley.

By the time he returned to Thebes in May 1818 (having, inter alia, made the first modern entry into the pyramid of Khaefre at Giza in the interim), Belzoni had developed plans for the comprehensive copying of the tomb of Sethy, with selected parts to be cast in wax, all with a view to an exhibition back in London. In Cairo, he had engaged (at Salt's expense) the physician and artist Alessandro Ricci (1792–1834)[15] to work on the project, work having already been underway for two months by the time Belzoni arrived.[16] Casting and drawing took a year, Ricci claiming to have worked eight- to twelve-hour days for seven months, without any companion for much of the time.

The casting is described by Belzoni as follows:

> The works at the tomb went on uncommonly well. By this time I had taken many impressions of the principal figures in basso relievo to my entire satisfaction. The wax alone, I found would not stand, as the climate did not permit it; but with wax, resin, and fine dust, I made an excellent composition. The greatest difficulty was to take the impression of the figure without injuring the colours of it. The figures as large as life I found to be in all a hundred and eighty-two: those of a smaller size, from one to three feet, I did not count, but they cannot be less than eight hundred. The hieroglyphics in this tomb are nearly five hundred, of which I took a faithful copy, with their colours; but they are of four different sizes, from one to six inches; so that I have been obliged to take one of each size, which makes nearly two thousand in all. Some wax I procured in the small towns of the country, but in such small quantities, that I was obliged to send down the Nile to Kenneh, Farshiout, and Girgeh.[17]

Although Belzoni is at pains throughout his account to emphasize his intent to avoid damaging the tomb, modern examination of the approximately 650 places where wax casting could be detected showed that it left behind both gross drips and a thin brownish-yellow flaky coating over the scenes in question.[18] On the other hand, it was determined that the paint remained intact under this layer, which had, in actuality, preserved it from other sources of damage.

In addition to his drawings for Belzoni, Ricci also produced a number of full-size tracings for William John Bankes (1786–1855),[19] who was traveling in Egypt at the time, and on whose behalf Belzoni had removed an obelisk from Philae (now at Kingston Lacy in Dorset, England). The question of on whose behalf some of the drawings were made became an issue when Belzoni (wittingly or unwittingly is not clear) took drawings which Ricci had made on his own account, leading to an accusation of theft. The matter was, however, resolved through the mediation of Salt.

Copying and casting of the tomb was completed before the end of the year, but by then the inner parts of the tomb were no longer in the 'perfect' state that visitors described at the time of its opening. These corridors and chambers had been protected from flooding by the well, but in his clearance of debris beyond, Belzoni had used it as a dump and also filled it to allow the calcite coffin to be removed:

> I must lament the unfortunate fate of some of the figures within this place. . . . [On 11 December 1818,] while I was absent up the Nile it happened to rain; the water, finding the entrance open, ran into the tomb, and though not much, was enough to occasion some damage to some of the figures. The dryness of the calcareous stone, which is more like lime itself than raw stone, absorbed the dampness, and consequently cracked in many places, particularly in the angles of the pillars on the doorways, &c.; and in one of the rooms there was a piece of stone detached, containing the upper part of three figures; and in another chamber, was a figure, which fortunately fell without much injury; though broken in three pieces, I saved it from farther destruction. I was not a little vexed to see such a thing happen. The damage done at that time was inconsiderable in a place of such an extent; but I fear, that in the course of a few years it will become much worse damage in the tombs as has been occasioned in any other way.[20]

An important issue was that the water penetrated into a shale layer directly underlying the limestone into which the tomb had been cut, causing it to expand and later contract as it dried out. By this mechanism it caused significant damage to the limestone layer above, into which the walls and ceilings of the tomb were cut (cf. fig. 102). The burial chamber and its annexes were particularly badly affected, the juncture between the limestone and shale layers coming just below its floor (see further pages 152, 154), with columns particular points of failure, J/E being almost wholly destroyed very early on (cf. fig. 96).[21]

Thus, as Belzoni feared, there began what would be a long-term degradation of the tomb, exacerbated by the loss of color from reliefs wet-squeezed by later visitors. The worst damage of this kind was done by the one hundred or so made using gypsum plaster—perhaps by Robert Hay (1799–1863)[22] and his associates during 1824–34—which both stripped off the paint and left behind disfiguring residues.[23] Papier-mâché wet squeezes, of which around 130 can be detected, left behind in some cases an incidentally protective layer, but others had the latter removed, taking paint with it. Above and beyond such damage was the cutting away of parts of the tomb by others in search of souvenirs, often not only removing the 'target' element but also destroying surrounding parts of the wall as 'collateral damage.' Cartouches were the especial target of such vandals, but other unusual features were also a magnet, for example part of the Opening of the Mouth text that mentioned Sethy's mother.

FIGURE 117 The Egyptian Hall.

FIGURE 118 A gallery of Belzoni's exhibition, showing the part-reconstruction of the upper pillared hall (F). Although poorly rendered by the artist, the visible pillar faces can be identified as Dc (?) and Bc, and the wall reliefs those from the east, south, and west walls (cf. fig. 85). To the left is the reconstruction of the antechamber (I).

This destruction manifestly increased the value of the copies made under Belzoni while the tomb was in pristine condition—incidentally the first time the decoration of a major Egyptian tomb had been copied in its entirety, and the last for some decades. As

well as these copies, Belzoni also took away most of the objects from the tomb, including the calcite coffin:

> Having put all things in readiness, and all the models of the tombs being embarked, I took out the celebrated sarcophagus, which gave me something to do (in consequence of its being so very slender and thin), lest it might break at the smallest touch of any thing: however, it was safely got out of the tomb and put in a strong case. The valley it had to pass to reach the Nile is rather uneven for more than two miles, and one mile of good soft sand and small pebbles. I had it conveyed on rollers all the way, and safely put on board.[24]

The same method was also used to bring the sarcophagus lid of Rameses III out of the Valley, joining the material from Sethy's tomb

FIGURE 119 Left and center: Ricci's copies of pillar faces Bc and Dd in chamber J; these pillars are now badly damaged, emphasizing the importance of these early reproductions. The coloring of the drawings erred, however, by substituting blue for yellow in a number of places, especially on the king's headdress. This error was corrected in the second set of watercolors, based on Ricci's work, but these were much cruder in execution (right). This example depicts one of the faces of the now-destroyed pillar E (see also fig. 96).

(plus Bankes's obelisk), which left Luxor by boat on 27 January 1819, arriving in Cairo on 18 February before being taken on to Rashid to embark for the United Kingdom.[25]

Sethy in London

Belzoni left Egypt for the last time in September 1819, arriving in London in March 1820, via his Italian home town of Padua. His book on his activities in Egypt was published later that year,[26] while on 1 May 1821 he opened an exhibition of his finds. This was held in the Egyptian Hall in Piccadilly, an exhibition and entertainment venue that had fortuitously been built in 1812 with an Egyptianizing façade and some internal features, thus fitting it ideally for Belzoni's show (fig. 117).

FIGURE 120 Part of Ricci's copy of the "races of man" section of the Fifth Hour of the Book of Gates, on the left wall of chamber F (cf. fig. 85), compared with its current state.

The exhibition included full-size recreations of the tomb's antechamber (I: Belzoni called it the "Hall of Beauties"), and part of the upper pillared hall, including all four pillars (F, fig. 118). In addition, there were casts of various other parts of the tomb's decoration and a one-sixth scale model of the entire tomb made up from Ricci's drawings, with added color, mounted on canvas and pinned to a wooden frame. The color had presumably been applied from notes, some error leading to the stripes of the *nemes* headdresses being made blue, rather than the correct yellow (fig. 119, left and center). A second set of colored drawings were subsequently prepared, presumably with the intention of running parallel exhibitions; it has been suggested that they were from the hand of Belzoni's assistant, James Curtin (1796–1825; see further page 137).[27] This set corrected the colors but was far inferior in quality to the original Ricci renderings (see fig. 119, right).

One problem that had confronted Belzoni from the moment of discovery was what to call the tomb. At first, he had used the discovery of the bovid in an inner chamber to dub the sepulcher the "Tomb of the Apis," but it was clear that the tomb was actually of a king. Unfortunately, in 1817 no one could yet satisfactorily read hieroglyphs, and although it was generally understood that cartouches enclosed royal names, there was no possibility of deciphering those in the tomb. However, by the time the exhibition was being planned, Thomas Young (1773–1829),[28] who had been working on the hieroglyphic script for some years, believed that he could read the cartouches of Sethy I (as available to him through the Piazza del Popolo obelisk) as "Psammis (son of) Necho"—that is, Psamtik II of the Twenty-sixth Dynasty.[29] This was essentially on the basis of the presence of the *p*-sign, which Young had correctly identified at the beginning of Sethy's nomen cartouche. This theory was bolstered by a belief that the four Nubians shown as part of the "races of man" sequence in the Fifth Hour of the Book of Gates in chamber F of the tomb (fig. 120) were "Ethiopian captives" from Psamtik II's Nubian campaign, known from the work of Herodotus, and the king's broader military prowess as attested in the Old Testament.[30]

On the other hand, while presenting his interpretation as one based on an "agreement of sacred and profane history," Young was also honest enough to note that the newly discovered Abydos King List of Rameses II (found by Bankes) had "only two kings intervening between this Psammis [Sethy I] and the Memnon of the ancients [Amenhotep III]". Further, he recognized that the presence of a Greek graffito mentioning (the real) Psammis (Psamtik II) at Abu Simbel suggested a much later date for the king than the temple. Young was also worried by Herodotus's statement that all kings of the dynasty to which Psammis belonged were buried at Sais, in the Delta. His conclusion was one echoed by many historians whose pet theory is opposed by inconvenient facts: "We may however hope that future researches will furnish us with materials that will be able to remove this and many other difficulties, which at present envelop the chronology of the kings of Egypt."[31]

However, Belzoni clearly did not share Young's reservations, announcing without qualification that:

according to Dr. Young's late discovery of a great number of hieroglyphics, he found the names of Nichao and Psammethis his son, inserted in the drawings I have taken of this tomb. It is the first time that hieroglyphics have been explained with such accuracy, which proves the doctor's system beyond doubt to be the right key for reading this unknown language; and it is to be hoped, that he will succeed in completing his arduous and difficult undertaking, as it would give to the world the history of one of the most primitive nations, of which we are now totally ignorant. Nichao conquered Jerusalem and Babylon, and his son Peammethis made war against the Ethiopians. What can be more clear than the above procession?[32]

As well as the casts and model of the tomb, the exhibition also included some actual fragments of the tomb, detached following the flooding, together with large quantities of other Egyptian material, including a pair of statues of Sekhmet, from the temple of Amenhotep III at Kom el-Hetan, two mummies (one of which Belzoni had unwrapped before a number of doctors earlier in the year), *shabtis*, canopic jars, a papyrus, and models of the various temples and of the Second Pyramid at Giza.[33] Unfortunately, Sethy's calcite coffin was still at Alexandria and would not arrive in London until September; only two fragments of its lid could thus be displayed in Piccadilly.

The exhibition opened on 1 May 1821 to considerable acclaim; as the *Literary Gazette* put it:

We congratulate the scientific, the learned, the literary, the lovers of art, and the curious, (which enumeration, we take it, embraces a large majority of the public) on the treat prepared for them in the Exhibition by Mr. Belzoni, which opens at the Egyptian Hall, Piccadilly, on Tuesday next. To describe this performance as singular, unique, extraordinary, is but faintly to portray it: to us it appears to be the most interesting and valuable spectacle that ever was conceived and executed. As a mere sight, it is strange and delightful; and as a study to the scholar and philosopher, it is replete with high and inexhaustible matter. It presents the earliest traces of art to the artist: the earliest subjects of comparative chronology to the antiquary in profane, and to the divine in sacred history; the earliest representations of various sciences to scientific enquirers; the earliest pictures of human kind, their occupations, superstitions, physical qualities, and moral attributes to man.[34]

The *New Monthly Magazine* particularly admired the reconstruction of the inner chambers:

The representation is so perfect that the beholder can easily participate in the feelings which are induced by the contemplation of those immense works, which must have occupied hundreds of labourers and artists for many years in the completion. A mere verbal description was sufficient to raise the highest interest; but a *facsimile* has infinitely more attractions, especially when the industry and perseverance indispensable to the success of such an undertaking are reflected upon. Mr. Belzoni's Exhibition has charms not only for the admirers of art and the lovers of antiquity, but those who are influenced by curiosity alone will find enough to astonish and delight them. The chambers, in which the original size and colour of the figures on the wall are exactly preserved, present much matter for speculation both to the mythologist and the historian.[35]

Nineteen hundred people visited on its first day alone; the exhibition closed for a while during the summer, but reopened in the autumn, running until May 1822. With the arrival of the calcite coffin in the United Kingdom, consigned at Salt's instruction to the British Museum, Belzoni approached the latter with a request that it might be transferred to the Egyptian Hall exhibition on a temporary basis. However, this did not occur, and the piece remained at the Museum, to become the subject of considerable wrangling and dispute (see below). Many of the contents of the exhibition were sold on 8 June 1822, the full-size casts of the chambers selling for £490; unfortunately, their subsequent history appears to be unknown.[36] The model of the tomb was, however, retained, and it was the centerpiece of a version of the exhibition that opened on Paris's Boulevard des Italiens during 1822. Although set up by Belzoni himself, its running was entrusted to James Curtin, who passed a fragment of the tomb's decoration to James Smithson (c.1765–1829), founder of the Smithsonian Institution, Washington, DC.

The calcite coffin had been lodged at the British Museum with a large group of material collected by Salt, including other items in which Belzoni had a direct pecuniary interest or owned outright (the latter including the Rameses III sarcophagus lid). As far as the calcite coffin was concerned, it had been agreed that Belzoni would get a share of any sale price that exceeded £2,000, and he claimed that he had an offer from an overseas buyer for £3,000. However, the Museum's trustees were unwilling to consider a figure of this magnitude, taking the view that its actual value was less than half of this. Indeed, the final price paid by the Museum for Salt's collection (less the calcite coffin), in 1823, was only £2,000. As a result, Salt's Second Collection, formed between 1819 and 1824, was sold to France for £10,000 and is now in the Louvre, including the coffer of Rameses III's sarcophagus. Belzoni presented the lid of that sarcophagus to Cambridge University's newly founded Fitzwilliam Museum in early 1823, the piece arriving on 31 March. By then, Belzoni was en route to Africa to seek the source of the River Niger; he never found it, dying and being buried at Gwato, Benin, on 3 December.

FIGURE 121 The façade of Sir John Soane's house in Lincoln's Inn Fields, London, and a nineteenth-century view of its interior, before the enclosure of the calcite coffin in its iron and glass case.

In February 1824, two months after its discoverer's death, with negotiations between Salt's agent and the British Museum over the calcite coffin making little progress, the architect (Sir) John Soane (1753–1837) registered an interest in being given first refusal, should the Museum not purchase. Negotiations dragged on into April, when the Museum finally decided not to buy the coffin; on the 13th, Soane's offer of £2,000 was accepted. The piece's future in the United Kingdom was thus secured, nullifying French, Bavarian, and Russian hopes of purchase, and British newspapers giving Soane's action a very positive response.

On 12 May, the back wall of Soane's house in Lincoln's Inn Fields, only a short distance from the British Museum, was breached to allow the calcite coffin to enter, being then lowered into place in the basement by ropes worked through the dome that lay in the roof directly above.[37] Here, it joined Soane's eclectic collections that he had been building up since he had moved to Lincoln's Inn Fields in 1794, expanding from his original house there into two adjoining properties (fig. 121).

In addition to the calcite coffin's trough, eighteen fragments of the lid were received, together with the single surviving fragment of the canopic chest (which was initially mistaken for the turn of the toes of the lid). Sixteen of the former could be reassembled into four groups, some of which were displayed for a while atop the trough although removed to glass cases in 1861. The trough itself was enclosed in a wheeled glazed iron case in 1866, although not before the blue pigment that had once filled the figures and hieroglyphs had been lost through environmental pollution and well-meaning, but most unfortunate, cleaning.

A complete facsimile of the decoration of the calcite coffin had been published two years previously[38] by Joseph Bonomi (1796–1878),[39] curator since 1861 of what had, in 1837, become the state-owned Sir John Soane's Museum. Bonomi had previously worked extensively in Egypt as a draftsman with or alongside all the major British explorers of Egypt since 1823,[40] as well as the Prussian expedition of 1842–44. By the 1860s he was one of the doyens of British Egyptology[41] and produced copies of the highest quality and fidelity that remain the basis for all subsequent studies of the inscriptions.[42] The letterpress to the volume was produced by Samuel Sharpe (1799–1881), a banker but self-taught in hieroglyphs and Coptic and who was a significant figure in British Egyptology for much of the nineteenth century, although the holder of a number of rather eccentric and outmoded views on historical and linguistic matters.

Thus, the name of the king was rendered in the publication as "Oimenepthah," and his date fixed "not necessarily earlier than B.C. 1175," with the view that the king died around 1147.[43] On the other hand, the book attempted to pick up every monument attributable to Sethy I, including sections on his Qurna memorial temple (called by them the temple of Errebek), the Hypostyle Hall at Karnak, the 'palace' at Abydos (also erroneously attributing the beginning of Rameses II's temple there to Sethy I), the Piazza del Popolo obelisk, and material in the British Museum. Alongside a cast from Karnak and two from KV17, and a contemporary private stela, one of the 'guardian statues' from the tombs of Rameses I (page 113) and Rameses IX (page 128) was erroneously attributed to Sethy's tomb.

Various further fragments of the calcite coffin lid have been picked up in the Valley of the Kings over the years, two being given to the Soane Museum in 1910 by the Bonn Egyptologist Alfred Wiedemann (1856–1936),[44] who had found them in 1906. Three pieces ended up in the British Museum, and one in Strasbourg. Further similar pieces have been found in more recent years, although as such calcite coffins were used by kings into the Twentieth Dynasty, it is not certain whether some without surviving names actually belong to Sethy I's lid.

Had Belzoni lived, there had been plans to exhibit the tomb model in other locations. However, the Paris show was not a financial success, and following Belzoni's death, his widow, Sarah (1783–1870),[45] together with Curtin, opened another version of the display on 3 April 1825 at 28 Leicester Square, with an avowed intention of raising funds for Belzoni's mother and other relatives back in Padua. To mark its opening, Soane held three receptions (on 23, 26, and 30 March) at his house, at which guests could view the calcite coffin, as well as the rest of Soane's collection. The events took place by lamplight, the coffin apparently having candles placed inside to give full effect to its translucence. Sarah Belzoni was present on the first evening, and on the second the guests included Prince Augustus Frederick, Duke of Sussex (1773–1843, son of George III), the prime minister, the Earl of Liverpool (1770–1828), and various other distinguished individuals. These spanned nobility to the world of arts and science: from the latter came the poet Samuel Taylor Coleridge (1772–1834) and the painter J.M.W. Turner (1775–1851). Curtin had planned to attend to describe the coffin to the Duke but was prevented by a sprained ankle. The final evening's attendees included Home Secretary (Sir) Robert Peel (1788–1850) and the future founding president of Argentina, Bernardino Rivadavia (1780–1845).

Sethy in Brussels, Jersey, Somerset, and Bristol

Sadly, in spite of this spectacular launch, the revived exhibition was not a success, the sudden death of Curtin in May probably contributing to this; indeed, in October, the models and casts were seized from Sarah for debt. She seems to have come to an agreement with her creditors, receiving a small allowance from them and moving to Brussels to live more economically, certainly residing there by April 1827.[46] She had with her at least some of the drawings from the two versions ('blue' and 'yellow') of the Sethy tomb model, plus a number of other antiquities and mementoes of her husband and their sojourn in Egypt.[47] In 1828 she issued a prospectus for a new set of eighty lithographs of images from Sethy's tomb, but this evidently failed to achieve the required two hundred subscribers.

Giovanni appears to have been a keen Freemason (joining the Royal Arch Chapter at St. James's in London in 1821), although he never made any mention of masonry in his surviving works; however, from 1843 onward, Sarah wrote a number of pieces on the subject, perhaps incorporating unpublished views of her husband.[48] In these, she claimed that the tomb of Sethy I was actually a subterranean masonic temple, in which "Pharaoh Ousirei, King of Egypt, is represented in the greater part of this tomb, as going through the ceremonies of initiation into the sublime mysteries of Masonry, etc."[49] This quotation comes from a paper of hers, dated October 1843, which was later printed in an 1880 book by her 1849 Brussels lodger,[50] the French–American physician John A. Weisse (1810–80), expounding that author's wide-ranging "ancient freemasonry" theories. Versions and summaries of the paper had, however, appeared in a number of masonic publications during the intervening years, as well as in newspaper articles.

Weisse also included images of scenes from the tomb in his volume, including that of the king before Osiris from the Book of Gates in hall F (shown in fig. 86). Sarah had described this as "The High Priest, Grand Master, or High Grand Master, represented in a Temple, seated on a throne of state," but Weisse's expanded interpretation called it a "group of Grand Master, Guide, Candidate, and Assistant" at a masonic initiation.[51] He then went on to opine that:

> modern Freemasonry had its prototype in the Masonic Temple of Seti I. and Rameses II.[52] [i.e. KV17], where applicants were initiated as Oriental and Occidental Masonic orders initiate now. Throughout the thirteen highly ornamented mystery chambers of the Seti and Rameses temple are nine different initiations, little differing from those we give in this epitome. The position of the hands of the Grand Master here, the right hand of the guide and candidate, as well as the posture of the assistant, look like an initiation to some Masonic degree. In vain will some Masons say these performances

FIGURE 122 Left: the gravestone of Sarah Belzoni in the Mont à l'Abbé cemetery, Jersey, Channel Islands; right: the memorial to Selina Belzoni Tucker and her sister Sarah, in Milton Road cemetery, Weston-super-Mare, Somerset, England.

belonged to Egyptian religious mysteries. No one but such as have not attentively looked at them will talk of religious rites and ceremonies. The attitudes, eyes, and faces of the individuals, the signs, emblems, and symbols around them, indicate anything but religion or devotion. There is nothing humble, devotional, or prayerful in their countenances or in their postures. The four or five initiatory groupings in the preceding ninth and tenth mystery chambers seem to indicate no religion. The last one, where the candidate comes before the Grand Master with raised hands, is so well known to Masons that it needs no explanation. Any brother who will take the trouble to go and see the beautiful illustrations of Belzoni's discoveries at the Astor Library, or come and look over the series presented to us by Mrs. Belzoni, may realize that the groupings and their surroundings were purely Masonic.

Although of course utterly wrong, these interpretations were long taken in some masonic circles to be accurate, adding another layer to the reception of Sethy I and his tomb into Western culture.[53]

Granted a British pension during 1851/52, Sarah moved to Jersey, Channel Islands, probably early in the 1860s, where she died on 12 January 1870 (fig. 122, left).[54] She left all her possessions to her unmarried goddaughter Selina Belzoni Tucker (1821–93), which included the last scraps of the Belzoni collection. Among these were the last surviving examples of the drawings of the tomb of Sethy I, numbering in all some 250 sheets. Selina had spent part of her life as a governess, including a period in Brussels, during which she presumably became better acquainted with her godmother. On Selina's death, in Weston-super-Mare, Somerset (fig. 122, right), the collection was bequeathed to her distant cousin Sarah Ann Wilson (neé Tucker, 1844–1921), who gave the collection to Bristol City Museum through the agency of her son, Charles Edward Wilson (b. 1872), in 1900. Loaned to the Musées royaux d'Art et Histoire in Brussels for an exhibition in 1935, a selection are periodically exhibited in Bristol and have been loaned for other shows, including bicentenary exhibitions in 1978 at Bristol Museum and the Italian Cultural Institute, London, as well as the two at Sir John Soane's Museum and at the Antikenmuseum, Basel, Switzerland, during 2017/18.

Decipherment, Destruction, and Discovery

While Young had been able to make meaningful hypotheses about the decipherment of hieroglyphs, his success was strictly limited, with the problematic results previously noted. However, in 1822, Jean-François Champollion (1790–1832)[55] published his initial results on the question, which, although incomplete and partially erroneous, promised a real prospect of a methodology by which hieroglyphic inscriptions could be read. His first comprehensive summary appeared in 1824, but although a number of kings'

FIGURE 123 The left wall of chamber Fa, showing the rough opening through to corridor G caused by the 1829 cutting-out of the doorjamb now in the Louvre (fig. 89, right).

FIGURE 124 Also removed from the tomb in 1829 was pillar face Aa from chamber Jb (BM EA855).

cartouches were correctly identified in this work, including those of Rameses II, Sethy I was not among them.

This was probably owing both to the corrupt state of Manetho apropos the placement and identity of his "Sethos," and also difficulties in separating out the elements of Sethy I's compound nomen—especially in his tomb, with its substitutions of Osiris for Seth. By 1829, however, Champollion had correctly isolated Sethy, although calling him "Ménéphtha Ier" ("Ménéphtha II" being Merenptah and "Ménéphtha III," Sethy II). The second part of the nomen was recognized, but read variously as "Osiréi," "Noubéi," "Athothéi," and "Amonéi."[56] The king was nevertheless correctly placed between Rameses I and II, in an essentially correct late Eighteenth–Nineteenth Dynasty sequence (missing, of course, the Amarna kings). The reading "Sethy" was finally determined by Richard Lepsius in 1835.

In 1828, Champollion had arrived in Egypt jointly leading a Franco–Tuscan expedition alongside Ippolito Rosellini (1800–43)[57] of Florence.[58] Early in 1829, he was in the Valley of the Kings, copying and making notes on the decorations of the then-open tombs, including, of course, that of Sethy I. However, while Belzoni had taken only copies and casts of the decoration of the tomb, Champollion and Rosellini resolved to take sections of relief back to Europe. Bonomi, much later custodian of Sethy's calcite coffin, then working at Thebes, learned of this and remonstrated in writing, invoking an implicit residual British protectorate over the tomb.[59] This was denied by Champollion, who had

permission from the Egyptian authorities and was of the opinion that the tomb was doomed to destruction and that removal of the reliefs in question was the only means of preserving them for posterity. The walls of the gate at the entrance to corridor G were accordingly cut away (fig. 123) and shipped to Florence and Paris (fig. 89); pillar face Jb/Aa was also removed at the same time and passed to the British Museum in 1837 via James Burton (1788–1862)[60] (fig. 124).[61]

Destruction within the tomb over the next few years cannot be traced in any detail, but eight fragments were given to the British Museum by (Sir) Gardner Wilkinson (1797–1875)[62] in 1834, on his return from twelve years in Egypt. By their random nature, these would appear to have become detached accidentally, as part of the 'natural' deterioration of the tomb since the 1818 flood. Wilkinson,

FIGURE 125 The temple of Sethy I at Abydos, as exposed by Auguste Mariette. This is one of a number of versions of a painting by Ernst Koerner (1846–1927), in this case dated 1888; it shows the temple before the roof was restored (cf. figs. 30, 31).

however, also contributed directly to the tomb's destruction, by making squeezes during 1826, as did the British collector Henry Stobart (1821–95)[63] during 1854–55.

Another 'scientific' removal occurred in 1845, when Carl Richard Lepsius (1810–84),[64] leading the great Prussian expedition to Egypt,[65] took away column face Ba from the burial chamber, for display in Berlin (fig. 96). By now the question of the reading of Sethy I's nomen had been resolved, as had the corruptions in the Manethonic lists for the Eighteenth/Nineteenth Dynasty transition.[66] Lepsius accordingly called the king "Sethos," following the convention of referring to Egyptian kings by a Greek form of their name where this approximated to their original Egyptian one. By then Sethy's principal standing monuments had almost all been visited and to some degree documented—even the remote chapel at Wadi Abbad (Belzoni had been there, as had contemporaries).

Excavations by Auguste Mariette (1821–81),[67] founder of the Egyptian Antiquities Service, uncovered most of Sethy's Abydos temple during 1863, with the majority of its inscriptions published in 1869. However, some of the largely uninscribed peripheral areas remained uncleared, and it was not until the twentieth century that work was completed (cf. page 151), with the lost parts of the roof later restored to match the largely intact inner parts.

The Lost Pharaoh

Nevertheless, Sethy's mummy still remained hidden in the Theban hills' tomb TT320; this would, however, soon also be revealed. The discovery was made by three brothers of a local Qurnawi family, Muhammad (d. 1926), Ahmed (d. 1918/19), and Husein Abd el-Rassul, either by accident or as part of a systematic search for tombs to rob (stories vary).[68] The date of their discovery is also unclear, perhaps in or before 1869, if a section of the papyrus of Queen Nedjmet donated by King Edward VII to the British Museum in 1903 was acquired by him while in Egypt that year. It was in any case certainly before March 1874, when objects from TT320 are definitely recorded as having been purchased by travelers; key members of the Abd el-Rassul family were reported as saying that the discovery had been made in the summer of 1871.

The Abd el-Rassuls had been selling off material from the tomb—principally deriving from the burials of the Twenty-first Dynasty—for a number of years before suspicion fell upon them. Under questioning, the brothers denied all knowledge, but, with the net closing, and with growing dissent between them, on 25 June 1881, the eldest, Muhammad, confessed in exchange for an amnesty. On 5 July, Emile Brugsch (1842–1930),[69] keeper of Cairo's Bulaq Museum and at that time the most senior Antiquities Service official actually in the country (it was holiday season), arrived in Luxor with Ahmed Kamal (1851–1923),[70] its secretary-interpreter, and an inspector from Giza, Thadeos Matafian; the next day they were guided to the tomb. There, close

FIGURE 126 The mummy of Sethy I, shown just after its unwrapping in 1886, displaying the damage to the abdomen caused by the tomb robbers who had stripped off its original bandages in search of jewelry (Cairo JE26213=CG61077).

to the entrance, they found the encoffined mummy of Sethy I.

Concerned for the security of both the tomb's contents and himself, Kamal, together with Matafian and Brugsch, spent the night gathering a three-hundred-strong workforce and on the morning of the 7th began to clear the deposit. Work was complete the following day, and the coffins, sewn up in sailcloth for their protection, were on the 9th taken down to the river for transport to Cairo. On the 14th, the Service's steamers arrived at Luxor, sailing the next day and arriving at the Museum's dock in Bulaq on the 21st.

The mummies and coffins subsequently went on temporary display at the Museum, split between the Central Gallery and Jewelry Gallery, although additional space to hold them was soon commissioned. This was opened in October 1882, but it was not until April 1886 that all the mummies and coffins were in glass cases.

Brugsch unwrapped the mummy of Thutmose III in July 1881, but its badly damaged state discouraged further unwrappings for the time being. However, after two queens were unwrapped after showing signs of deterioration in 1883 and 1885, Gaston Maspero (1846–1916),[71] director of the Antiquities Service, decided in 1886 that a number of the most important bodies should be unwrapped in a planned manner. This was begun on 1 June, when Rameses II and III were dealt with in the presence of Khedive Tewfik (r. 1879–92) himself.

Sethy I was divested of his wrappings on the 9th, along with the Seventeenth Dynasty king Taa (fig. 126). The process was carried out by Maspero, Brugsch, Urbain Bouriant (1849–1903, assistant keeper),[72] Hervé Bazil (administrator in the Antiquities Service and Maspero's half-brother), Jan Insinger (1854–1918, a dealer and photographer),[73] and Daniel Fouquet (1850–1914, a medical doctor).[74] The audience included General Sir

Frederick Stephenson (1821–1911, commander in chief of the British Army of Occupation [since 1883]), Garnier de Heldewier (Belgian consul general), General Comte della Sala Pasha and his wife, and Eugène Grébaut (1846–1915, the new director general of the Antiquities Service).[75]

The set of bandages and shrouds were arranged in the same way as on the mummy of Ramses II; at about half of the total depth, we learned from a double inscription in two lines drawn in black ink that in Year 9, the second month of "*peret* on the 16th day we repaired King Menmaatre (Sethy I), l.p.h." Another inscription written on one of the strips adds that the linen employed in the wrapping had been made by the First Prophet of Amun Menkheperre in Year 6, which gives us the last restoration undergone by the conqueror's mummy. The body has approximately the same appearance as that of Rameses II. Long, emaciated, yellow-black, arms crossed on the chest, the genitals separated by the aid of a sharp instrument.

FIGURE 127 The Egyptian Museum in Midan Tahrir, the home of the mummy of Sethy I since 1902, except for the period 1931–36.

The head was covered with a thick mask of thin linen, blackened by tar, which had to be removed with a chisel. M. Alexandre Barsanti, who was charged with this delicate operation, brought out of this shapeless mass the most beautiful head of a mummy yet seen at the Museum. The sculptors of Thebes and Abydos did not flatter Pharaoh when they gave him the delicate, sweet and smiling profile that travelers admire: the mummy has after thirty-two centuries the same expression as when alive. What strikes first when we compare it to that of Rameses II is the amazing resemblance between father and son: nose, mouth, chin, the traits are the same, but thinner, smarter, more human in the father. Sethy I is like the idealized type of Ramses II. He must have died in old age, the head is shaved, the eyebrows are white and the state of the body suggest that sixty years old had been well passed, which confirms the opinion of the scholars who attribute to him a very long reign. The body is healthy, vigorous, yet the knotty fingers bear obvious traces of arthritis; both teeth that we see under the resin that fills the mouth are white and well preserved.[76]

Returned to the trough of his wooden coffin, the unwrapped mummy went on display at Bulaq.[77] By 1889, it was suffering from exposure to the damp air of the riverside location of the Museum,[78] being observed with its face covered with a thin layer of salt.[79] The mummy was moved later that year, together with the rest of the museum collection, to a former palace in Giza, which opened on 12 January 1890, as the temporary home for the institution pending the construction of a purpose-built museum on what is today Tahrir Square in Cairo (fig. 127). This building was completed in 1902, Sethy and most of the other royal mummies being placed in the western gallery at the rear of the upper floor of the new building (as of 2018 designated Gallery 7, and housing part of the Tutankhamun collection).

In their new Cairene location, Sethy and the mummies were again examined, this time by Grafton Elliot Smith (1871–1937),[80] Professor of Anatomy at Cairo Medical School, leading to their publication in 1912 in a volume of the *General Catalogue of the Egyptian Museum*.[81] In 1928, a general decision was taken to no longer display unwrapped mummies, and thus such bodies were either placed back in their coffins, which remained on display with their lids closed, or moved to a special room, access to which required Ministerial permission. The space vacated by the royal mummies was taken over by the newly arrived shrines that had surrounded Tutankhamun's sarcophagus.

The mummies' withdrawal from view coincided with the start of work on a controversial pharaonic-styled mausoleum (fig. 128) to hold the body of the politician Sa'd Zaghlul (1859–1927).[82] However, by the time it was completed in 1931, Zaghlul's party, the Wafd, was out of power, and the now-incumbent People's Party prime minister, Isma'il Sidqi (1875–1950), proposed to make it into a national pantheon, rather than a tomb for just one man. Thus, at the end of 1931, Sethy and the other principal royal

FIGURE 128 During 1931–36, the principal royal mummies were housed in the mausoleum intended for Sa'd Zaghlul.

mummies were moved to the mausoleum. However, with the death of King Fuad I (r. 1917–36), an opponent of Zaghlul, in April 1936, and the return of a Wafd government the following month, the mummies were removed and Zaghlul reburied in his mausoleum in June, after his widow had been given a legal guarantee that Zaghlul's would in future be the only body ever to lie there.

The mummies were returned to the Museum and placed in various storerooms. It was not until 1945 that a dedicated space was provided for the royal mummies, in Gallery 52 in the southwest corner. Here, they were the subject of x-ray examination in 1967 by a mission from the Universities of Michigan and Alexandria. Sethy's images revealed some beads and an Eye of Horus amulet still embedded in his remaining wrappings— the latter on his left arm and possibly of gold, like parallel items found on the mummy of Tutankhamun.[83] Physically, postmortem fractures were noted and the king's dental health assessed as showing "Moderate-Extensive" attrition, with "Fair-Poor" periodontal health (contrasting with "Extensive" and "Severe" in the mummies of Rameses II and Merenptah).[84] Sethy's age at death was assessed as "35–40,"[85] although doubts now exist as to the validity of modern aging criteria to premodern remains.[86]

The mummies remained on display there until 1981, when President Anwar Sadat (1918–81) ordered that the gallery be closed, in the future to be accessible only by special permission. Sethy and his companions thus languished there behind closed doors until 1994, when he and the other Eighteenth and Nineteenth Dynasty kings were conserved and partly rewrapped—with their faces left exposed—before being moved to new high-specification cases in Gallery 56 at the opposite end of the south range of the museum. Gallery 52 was later refurbished to contain the later royal and high-priestly mummies.

At the end of the 2000s, a number of mummies, including that of Sethy I, were examined using computed tomography.[87] On the basis of this new imaging, the king's age was pushed up to "40–50" and his height computed (required owing to the breaking of the body at the neck and lower back) to be "169 cm ± 4.4 cm" (5 feet 6½ inches ± 1¾ inches). It could be seen that the brain had been removed through the nose and the skull filled with resin and linen. The king showed minor degenerative changes to his hip joints, with minor tooth wear, and had suffered the loss of one tooth during his lifetime.

Sethy I remains in Gallery 56 at the time of writing, although there have been for some years plans for all the royal mummies to be moved to the new National Museum of Egyptian Civilization (NMEC) in Fustat, in southern Cairo. Here, they are planned to lie in a subterranean complex intended to evoke an ancient tomb. However, while the first phase of the NMEC was opened in 2017, future timescales remain unclear, and it may be some years before Sethy makes his next move in a distinctly restless posthumous career.

FIGURE 129 A steam pump being used to free the Osireion of water during the Egypt Exploration Society's excavations in 1926 (cf. figs. 42 and 43).

Archaeology and Epigraphy

In the spring of 1883, a team led by Eugène Lefébure (1838–1908),[88] director of Mission archéologique française in Egypt, undertook the copying of Sethy I's tomb. The work was undertaken as part of a broader project to summarily document all the tombs in the Valley of the Kings, with the tombs of Sethy and Rameses IV singled out for complete copying in near facsimile. Many of the drawings of Sethy's tomb were undertaken by Urbain Bouriant (see page 145) or Victor Loret (1859–1946),[89] in some cases based on earlier published copies of Belzoni, Champollion, Rosellini, and Lepsius; the original Ricci copies, however, were apparently unknown or inaccessible at the time. The volume covering Sethy's tomb was published in 1886.

A decade and a half later, the Osireion was revealed for the first time since antiquity. Although Mariette had cleared most of the Abydos temple in 1863, he had not touched the area directly to the west, and it was here, at the beginning of the twentieth century, that a team from the University College London–based Egyptian Research Account carried out new work, including revealing the temple's western enclosure wall and gate. However, in the space between this and the rear of the temple, a hollow in the sand was observed, which turned out to be the Merenptah-decorated antechamber of the Osireion. This was cleared and recorded by Margaret Murray (1863–1963)[90] and Hilda Petrie (1871–1956)[91] during 1901–02,[92] as was the entrance passageway, but work had to be terminated without being able to penetrate the main body of the structure. Excavations were resumed by the Egypt Exploration Fund (from 1919, Society [EES]) under Edouard Naville (1844–1926)[93] in 1912, most of the monument having been revealed by the time that work was stopped in the spring of 1915. Completion of the clearance and recording of the Osireion was carried out under the direction of Henri Frankfort (1897–1954)[94] between 1925 and 1930, with the final publication coming out in 1933 (fig. 129).

From 1928, the main Abydos temple was the subject of a joint EES–University of Chicago project to copy the decoration in full color, with generous funding from the American philanthropist John D. Rockefeller, Jr. (1874–1960).[95] The work was carried out by Amice Calverley (1896–1959)[96] and Myrtle Broome (1888–1978)[97] until 1937, four volumes eventually being published. Parts of the temple still, however, remain without proper publication, in spite of field work having been carried out during the 1980s by John Baines (b. 1946), under the continuing auspices of the EES.

Saving the Tomb

During 1903/4, the first significant efforts were made to arrest the alarming deterioration of Sethy I's tomb. At the end of that season, Howard Carter (1874–1939),[98] Antiquities Service Inspector General for Upper Egypt, penned the following report:

> 1. *State.* – For very many years, the state of this tomb has been bad. The limestone rock in which it is hewn and sculptured is, though of a fine nature, very shaley and full of natural cracks which in many cases have become disintegrated from age; these parts of the surface have scaled and fallen away. This condition has not been improved by former explorers and antiquity hunters. The painted sculptures have been defaced by making wet squeezes. The sculptured walls have been hacked indiscriminately, to gouge out cartouches as well as pretty pieces of reliefs. Parts of columns and door-jambs, which acted as supports, have

been removed. The ceiling is totally blackened by smoke from torches and candles.

In reading through Belzoni's interesting account of his discovery of this tomb, in 1817, and his description of its beautifully decorated walls and ceiling, one cannot but think that it must then have been in a perfect condition.

2. *Disintegration*. – Of late years, each season has recorded small falls of stone from its ceilings, walls, and columns. On February 11th 1901, in the vestibule J, of the [crypt], a considerable portion of the centre of the ceiling and the much dilapidated column [J/E] collapsed, leaving dangerous cracks and pieces hanging, which had to be temporarily supported by wooden strutts. In the beginning of April 1902, the end wall of the [crypt] subsided, bringing down with it a portion of the painted ceiling and wall over the doorway leading to the uninscribed chamber [Jc], and also causing in the left-hand side wall fissures to open and slight displacement of the side of the doorway leading to the offering chamber [Jb]. The portions of the ceilings, walls, and columns that fell broke into a myriad fragments, some of which I fear can never be properly replaced. Perhaps, one of the reasons why the lower chambers of this tomb have suffered so much from falls, is owing to the fact that the limestone stratum abruptly stops at about 0 m. 60 cent. above the floor and a softer *tafle* stratum begins. This lower stratum has by no means the sustaining power of the upper. Then, again, the end wall of the large vaulted chamber has beneath it a tunnel excavated in the *tafle* stratum and leading to sepulchral chambers below; thus, a large portion of its length is unsupported, and its strength is not enhanced by the fact of there being another chamber behind it.

3. *Reparation*. – The flaking of pieces of rock from different parts of the surfaces cannot be prevented, I fear, without disfiguring the tomb altogether, but a great deal of further large breakages can be avoided by supporting the rock where it has not sufficient means of carrying its own weight.

Mr. Robert Mond, who was here when the last subsidence occurred, in April 1902, very kindly gave, as I have already mentioned in my report of that year, the sum of [£]50 towards the repair of this tomb. He also lent me his valuable assistance in making out a project for the work, which began in the early part of May, after I had reported it to my Director. I began in the [crypt] by first carefully strutting up the wall that had subsided, then by clearing away the rubbish and loose rock beneath, at the entrance of the tunnel, making there a level platform as a foundation to receive two masonry jambs for an arch to support that wall; the arch was inserted to obtain enough strength to support the weight of the wall and, at the same time, to allow access to the tunnel leading to the chambers below. The wall over the doorway leading to chamber ([Jc]) was treated in the same manner, so that a similar supporting arch could be made giving access to that chamber.

When clearing away the rubbish in the tunnel [K], I found many uninscribed carefully shaped slabs of stone, that had served to form a staircase and slide for funerary equipment to the sepulchral chambers. These stones were much displaced, and being in want of a good building material for the jambs of the arches, I was compelled to use them for that purpose. For the arches themselves I procured several thousand European red-bricks from Erment.

The wall over the tunnel was lifted up to its former level by means of screw-jacks, thus closing up the cracks in the rock while replacing all fallen fragments which could be reinstated. The arches, of one metre in thickness, were then built with sufficient masonry upon them to hold the wall in place. There being vertical cracks in the thickness of this wall I put two iron clamps on the end to prevent them from opening; to assure the arch against any undue side pressure in the doorway of chamber [Jc], I built in with the masonry one of the heavy wooden cross strutts that were placed between the two door-jambs.

In the case of the displacement of the side wall, dividing the [crypt] and offering chamber [Jb], the dislocated pieces were put back in position and held in their places by brick masonry built underneath, the bad rock being cut away to receive the masonry. All round this [crypt], the interval between the floor level and the bottom of the good stratum of limestone, was originally faced with a limestone casing, the soft rock or *tafle* having been cut back to receive it. This was done for two reasons, to support the face of the limestone above, and to make the whole wall uniform. A great deal of this facing having in course of time fallen, I replaced it with solid red-brick masonry.

A wooden railing was put round the opening leading to the tunnel to prevent visitors, from falling in.

From the ceiling in the vestibule I removed the wooden supports put there temporarily, and replaced them by iron girders supported by four iron columns; repairing at the same time the three columns [J/A, J/B, and J/D], with red-brick masonry. I also strengthened column [J/C] by two iron bands, there being a vertical crack down its centre. The broken door-jambs of the chambers [H] and [I] were also repaired with cement.

Besides the above repairs many odd jobs were done for the preservation of this tomb, including the patching up of one of the columns in the upper chambers, and painting the whole of the new work so as to be unobtrusive.

Outside, the entrance staircase being so irregular and dangerous to visitors, l rebuilt the left-hand half with cement, faced the treads with timber, and put a wooden rail at the side.[99]

The tomb was recorded photographically by Harry Burton (1879–1940),[100] under the auspices of the Metropolitan Museum of Art, New York, during 1921–28, providing a comprehensive record of its state at the time (for example, fig. 88).[101]

The Quest of Sheikh Ali

The first 9.7 meters of "tunnel" beyond the crypt had been lined with brick arches by Carter as part of his conservation efforts, but he had made no attempt to investigate the passages beyond. Belzoni had penetrated some ninety meters, but by the 1840s, only half that length was accessible to Wilkinson, and by 1959 it was only possible to access the first twenty-five meters or so.[102]

However, in 1960 an attempt was made to clear and reach the end of the mysterious "tunnel." This was not by professional Egyptologists but by Sheikh Ali Abd el-Rassul (d. 1987), a hotelier and a scion of the family that had found TT320 and the mummy of Sethy I. He nevertheless, aided by a press campaign and private donations, managed to obtain permission to undertake the work in the hope of finding the "treasure" he believed to lie at the end. The first forty-five meters beyond Carter's arches was properly cleared and equipped with a supporting infrastructure, but given the labor required to carry the excavated debris not only from there up to the crypt, but also then through the tomb to the surface, the material removed from further down was deposited in the previously cleared area, clearing only a narrow tunnel in an attempt to reach the end.

Safety concerns for the workers led to the Egyptian antiquities authorities requiring work to be terminated in the spring of 1961, by which time Sheikh Ali had penetrated 136 meters—although it later proved that for around the last thirty meters he had been cutting through virgin rock (albeit so crumbly that it was all but indistinguishable from debris) above the actual line of the passage. Apart from a survey by the Theban Mapping Project in 1979, which did no more than record the space as left by Sheikh Ali, the "tunnel" would remain abandoned until the following century.

Modern Times

In spite of Carter's efforts at the beginning of the century, deterioration continued, with additional metal supports being added in the columned section of the burial chamber in 1981, and in the vaulted crypt in 1988 following a further collapse, and again in 1991. During 1998–99, a series of conservation studies were carried out in the tomb by the American Research Center in Egypt (ARCE), which provided a more refined view of the geology of the tomb.[103] This showed strata of the Thebes Formation's limestones lying upon the Esna Formation's alternating layers of shale and white marl (Carter's "tafle"), the transition coming directly below the floor of the antechamber and the outer part of the burial chamber. It was the effect of water on the latter that had caused the start of deterioration of the tomb, exacerbated by large numbers of rock joints running transversely across the axis, with major collapses coinciding with the Esna Formation intruding into the crypt, repaired by Carter's brickwork.

The studies also revealed that 880 places in the tomb showed the effect of squeezes, sometimes with a scene having been squeezed on multiple occasions (cf. pages 129 and

FIGURE 130 Comparison of the 'as now' replica of chamber I and the pillared portion of chamber J, as displayed at the Antikenmuseum, Basel, during 2017/18 (top), and the 'as found' restored reconstruction of chamber I that also formed part of the same exhibition (bottom).

144). Other damage had been done by well-intentioned, but inappropriate, attempts at cleaning, conservation, and restoration.

Given the damage to the tomb, and the further deterioration exacerbated by ongoing tourist visits, the sepulcher was closed to general visitors in 1991. However, after further conservation and the installation of new LED lighting, it was reopened in 2017 with a special entry fee of 1,000 Egyptian pounds (at the time of writing equivalent to approximately US$57)—in addition to the normal Valley entry fee of 160 Egyptian pounds.

A decade before the reopening, a final attempt was made to properly clear the "tunnel," a team from the Supreme Council of Antiquities initiating work under the direction of Zahi Hawass (b. 1947) in September 2007.[104] This followed on from an initial investigation in 2002, which allowed the development of plans for full clearance. Between November 2007 and July 2008, excavations had reached Gallery K3, recovering a number of *shabtis* of Sethy I, plus a piece of the lid of the calcite coffin and fragments from the walls of the tomb. By the end of the October 2008–July 2009 season, clearance had reached the end of K6, below the point where Sheikh Ali had terminated his work, and thus was now in a part of the tomb never seen in modern times. A final season from November 2009 to March 2010 cleared K7 to the unfinished end of K10—clearing up the final mystery of KV17.

At the time of its closure it was proposed that KV17, as well as other popular but vulnerable tombs, in particular those of Nefertiry and Tutankhamun, should have exact replicas produced and made available to visitors as an alternative. The first such replica, produced by Factum Arte, of the tomb of Tutankhamun, was opened close to the former house of Howard Carter, just north of the road to the Valley of the Kings in April 2014.

Trial work having been carried out during 2001–02,[105] full-scale scanning of the tomb of Sethy I was begun in 2016, under the auspices of the Theban Necropolis Preservation Initiative, with the expectation that it would take at least five years to complete.[106] The first fruit of the work has been a complete reconstruction of chamber I and the outer section of J, which, together with a completely restored version of the former, was first displayed in an exhibition at the Antikenmuseum Basel, Switzerland, from October 2017 to May 2018 (fig. 130). This also included a 3D-printed replica of the calcite coffin. It is intended that a complete reconstruction of the tomb will eventually join that of Tutankhamun at Thebes West. The project, under the academic leadership of the University of Basel, also involved the cataloging and scanning of now-detached fragments—including a number found in recent years during the University's work in the Valley—and the reconstruction of damaged walls for the replica, where necessary with reference to the Ricci and other historic copies.[107]

Two centuries on from its discovery, the tomb of Sethy I remains a focus of Egyptological research, as well as serving as an object lesson in the difficulty of conserving monuments once uncovered. Even in its mutilated form, the tomb remains an icon of ancient Egyptian art and architecture, as does the king's Abydos temple, his conception of the Great Hypostyle Hall at Karnak, and even his mummy, generally lauded as the most handsome of its kind. Sethy I has thus experienced a notable modern afterlife, although perhaps not with the level of popular recognition of the global 'stars' of today's Egyptophilia, headed by Sethy's son, Rameses II, and the members of the Amarna royal family. The discovery of his tomb also marked an epoch in the reception of ancient Egypt by modern British society, Belzoni's exhibition being perhaps the direct ancestor of the 'blockbuster' shows that in more recent years have done so much to shape the wider audience's perceptions of the ancient world. Indeed, the names of Belzoni and Sethy now seem inextricably linked—giants of their world in the widest of senses.

CHRONOLOGY

LE = Lower Egypt only; UE = Upper Egypt.
All New Kingdom and Third Intermediate Period dates
are based on the scheme set out in Dodson 2012; in any
case, all are more or less conjectural prior to 690 BC.
Parentheses indicate a co-ruler.

EARLY DYNASTIC PERIOD

Dynasty 1	3050–2810 BC
Dynasty 2	2810–2660

OLD KINGDOM

Dynasty 3	2660–2600
Dynasty 4	2600–2470
Dynasty 5	2470–2360
Dynasty 6	2360–2195

FIRST INTERMEDIATE PERIOD

Dynasties 7/8	2195–2160
Dynasties 9/10 (LE)	2160–2040
Dynasty 11a (UE)	2160–2065

MIDDLE KINGDOM

Dynasty 11b	2065–1994
Dynasty 12	1994–1780
Dynasty 13	1780–1650

SECOND INTERMEDIATE PERIOD

Dynasty 14 (LE)	1700–1650
Dynasty 15 (LE)	1650–1535
Dynasty 16 (UE)	1650–1590
Dynasty 17 (UE)	1585–1540
Ahmose the Elder	
Taa	
Kamose	–1540

NEW KINGDOM

Dynasty 18

Ahmose I	1540–1516
Amenhotep I	1516–1496
Thutmose I	1496–1481
Thutmose II	1481–1468
Thutmose III	1468–1415
(Hatshepsut	1462–1447)
Amenhotep II	1415–1386
Thutmose IV	1386–1377
Amenhotep III	1377–1337
Akhenaten	1337–1321
(Smenkhkare	1325–1323)
(Neferneferuaten	1322–1319)
Tutankhamun	1321–1312
Ay	1312–1308
Horemheb	1308–1278

Dynasty 19

Rameses I	1278–1276
Sethy I	1276–1265
Rameses II	1265–1200
Merenptah	1200–1190
Sethy II	1190–1185
(Amenmeses [UE]	1189–1186)
Siptah	1185–1178
Tawosret	1178–1176

Dynasty 20

Sethnakhte	1176–1173
Rameses III	1173–1142
Rameses IV	1142–1136
Rameses V	1136–1132
Rameses VI	1132–1125
Rameses VII	1125–1118
Rameses VIII	1118–1116
Rameses IX	1116–1098
Rameses X (UE)	1098–1095
Rameses XI	1110–1095 (LE)
	+ 1095–1078 (UE)

THIRD INTERMEDIATE PERIOD

Dynasty 21

Herihor (UE)	1078–1065
Nesibanebjed I (LE)	1078–1053
Amenemnesut (UE?)	1065–1049
Panedjem I (UE)	1063–1041
Pasebkhanut I	1049–999
Amenemopet	1001–992
Osorkon the Elder	992–985
Siamun	985–867
Pasebkhanut II	967–941
Dynasty 22	943–736
Dynasty 23	736–666
Dynasty 24	734–721
Dynasty 25	754–656

SAITE PERIOD

Dynasty 26	664–525

LATE PERIOD

Dynasty 27	525–404
Dynasty 28	404–399
Dynasty 29	399–380
Dynasty 30	380–342
Dynasty 31	342–332

HELLENISTIC PERIOD

Dynasty of Macedonia	332–310
Dynasty of Ptolemy	310–30

ROMAN PERIOD 30 BC–AD 395

NOTES

Notes to Chapter 1

1   See Dodson 2014a: 1–80.

2   For an overview of this period, and discussions of key points, see Dodson 2014a: 81–136 and 2018: 1–52.

3   Two female stillborns were found in Tutankhamun's tomb, but although generally assumed to be the offspring of the king and Ankhesenamun, genetic analysis has not confirmed this.

4   See Dodson 2018: 114–15 on an alleged "first wife."

5   Cairo JE44863–4: Porter and Moss 1972: 188[584]; Delvaux 1992.

6   For the convention of distinguishing homonyms by the use of letters, see Dodson and Hilton 2010: 39.

7   See Hope and Ashten 2017.

8   Chicago OI 11456 (Cruz-Uribe 1978; Malek 2012: 247).

9   Martin 1989: 57, 84–85, pl. 53–54, 96–97.

10 Moran 1992: 11 (bringing gifts from Amenhotep III from Kadashman-Enlil of Babylon), 292–94 (at Akka), 331 (bringing slaves from Jerusalem to Egypt).

11 Khartoum 2690 (Porter and Moss 1952: 191).

12 Te Velde 1967.

13 Cairo JE60539 (Porter and Moss 1934: 23; Kitchen 1968–90: II, 287–88[71]; 1993–2014: II, 116–17[71]; 1993–99: 168–72[71]); on this and Paramessu's broader family background, see also: Gaballa and Kitchen 1968; Goedicke 1981; van Dijk in Martin 1997: 60–62; and Brand 2000: 336–43.

14 Winlock 1921; 1937.

15 See Dodson 2018: 130–32 for a full discussion.

16 Kitchen 1968–90: I, 1–5.

17 Kitchen 1968–90: I, 110–11[54]; 1993–2014: I, 93–94[54]; 1993–99: I, 93–94[54].

18 See Brand 2000: 310–12.

19 For these dates, see Brand 2000: 300–302.

20 Porter and Moss 1960–64: 534–35.

Notes to Chapter 2

1   For a compendium, see Von Beckerath 1999.

2   The term would later be used by Rameses XI to mark a new era, following civil strife under Rameses IX and X (see Dodson 2012: 9–10).

3   Jánosi 2010.

4   Martin 1997.

5   Kitchen 1968–90: II, 844–47[I]; 1993–2014: II, 550–52[I]; 1993–99: II, 549–57[I].

6   Porter and Moss 1960–64: 769; Kitchen 1993–99: II, 554–55; Leblanc 1989: pl. ccxii–iv.

7   Leblanc 1993/94: 92–94; Leblanc and Esmoingt 2014.

8   Kitchen 1968–90: II, 665–67[254, C]; 1993–2014: II, 446–47[254, C]; 1993–99: II, 438–41[254, C].

9   pLiverpool M11162 [pMayer A] (Kitchen 1968–90: VI, 811; 1993–2014: VI, 560), dated to Year 1 of the *whm-nswt*, corresponding to Year 19 of Rameses XI.

10 Sourouzian 1983; Kitchen 1993–99: II, 337, 569–70.

11 If she were a daughter of Rameses II (for which there is no support from any of the extant princess processions in Rameses's temples), she would have been one of his younger ones, with no obvious reason for her to be associated with her, probably then-dead, grandmother. Likewise, the other daughters who Rameses

II espoused were among his older ones, born of his original Great Wives Nefertiry and Isetneferet, which would not have been the case with Henutmire. None of these problems exist if Henutmire were Rameses's sister—perhaps considerably younger and perhaps, unlike Tia, not yet married when he came to the throne. Indeed, her appearance as a Great Wife after Year 34 (Kitchen 1993–99: II, 569) may reflect that, after the demise of Nefertiry and Isetneferet, Rameses decided to promote the last surviving female member of the family of his own generation, his sister Henutmire, to the status of Great Wife.

12   Porter and Moss 1960–64: 768–69; Leblanc 1988; 1989: pl. cci–vi.

13   Cairo JE60137 (Porter and Moss 1960–64: 772).

14   On a wall of the funerary chapel of an Apis bull at Saqqara (Dodson 1990: 87–88).

15   Dodson 2018: 13–17.

16   Dodson 2018: 98–99.

17   For a history of the topic and a discussion, see Brand 2000: 312–32.

18   Kitchen 1968–90: II, 323–336[103]; 1993–2014: II, 162–74[103]; 1993–99: II, 191–97[103].

19   Porter and Moss 1972: 348[19].

20   See discussion in Dorman 1988: 18–45.

21   On the king's posthumous deification, see Gaber 2013.

22   For Karnak, see Brand 2000: 201–19, for the memorial temple, 234–49.

23   Brand suggests (2000: 327) that the activities depicted included the Irem campaign of Sethy's Year 8 (see page 66); certainly there is no mention of Sethy I anywhere in the Beit el-Wali temple.

24   Given in a graffito at Elephantine (Brand 2000: 269–70).

25   In his *Inscription Dédicatoire*, l.53–56 (Kitchen 1968–90: II, 328; 1993–2014: II, 168).

26   Although evidence for such coregencies seems secure, some have doubted even their existence: see the debate between Delia (1979; 1982) and Murnane (1991).

27   For a discussion, see Dodson 2014b.

28   For which, see Murnane 1977.

29   Hatshepsut alongside Thutmose III and Neferneferuaten under Akhenaten, and possibly Tutankhamun as well.

30   In the case of the alleged co-rule of Thutmose III and Amenhotep II, where a note of the latter's accession day is a suspiciously exact two months before his father's documented death day. An error in writing the season name in either document would be enough to wipe out the sole objective evidence for a coregency between the two kings: all other data put forward in support of co-rule is of the similar equivocal kind presented in favor of the alleged Sethy I/Rameses II association (and others; for example, Amenhotep III/IV).

31   For which, see Dodson 2014a: 127–29.

32   For Sethy I's restoration activity, see Brand 2000: 45–118.

33   Brand 1999.

34   pRollin [BibNat] 213 (Kitchen 1968–90: I, 279–80; 1993–2014: I: 229–31; 1993–99: 184).

35   Löhr 1975: 146–47, 169–70.

36   Stannish, forthcoming.

37   Brand 2000: 128–33.

38   Listed in Brand 2000: 133–46, 298.

39   For Memphite material of Sethy I, see Brand 2000: 146–50.

40   Mariette 1857: 12; Dodson 2005: 77.

41   Porter and Moss 1974–81: 664–65, 716–17.

42   Porter and Moss 1939: 1–27; Calverley and Broome 1933–58; Brand 2000: 155–73; David 2016.

43   Porter and Moss 1939: 29–31; Brand 2000: 174–78.

44   For which see Dodson 1997/98.

45   Brand 2000: 178–83.

46   Kitchen 1968–90: II, 323–36[103]; 1993–2014: II, 162–74[103]; 1993–99: II, 191–97[103]; Spalinger 2009.

47   Translation after Kitchen 1993–2014: II, 165–68.

48   Reasons of space probably explain the omission of much of the First Dynasty from the list of kings in the Saqqara tomb of Tjenry (Porter and Moss 1974–81: 666), rather than the historically substantive reasons sometimes opined.

49   Brand 2000: 183–88.

50   Kitchen 1968–90: I, 342–50[XXIII]; 1993–2014: I, 278–86[XXIII]; 1993–99: I, 236–42[XXIII].

51   On the westward extension of the Karnak complex as the river retreated, see Bunbury, Graham, and Hunter 2008; for the subsequent history of building in the area, see Brand 2000: 192–219.

52   Porter and Moss 1972; Nelson 1981.

53   Brand 2000: 219–27.

54   Kitchen 1968–90: I, 326[XV]; 1993–2014: I, 264[XV]; 1993–99: I, 218–20[XV].

55   Brand 2000: 249–56.

56   Porter and Moss 1960–64: 1–5; Mahmoud 2011.

57   Brand 2000: 279–82.

58   Brand 2000: 262–65.

59   Found in September 2018, the stela seems to mention events during the reign of Horemheb (<https://www.livescience.com/63738-temple-engravings-of-warrior-pharaoh.html>).

60   Brand 2000: 266–75.

61   W.V. Davies 2001.

62   For Sethy's Nubian attestations, see Brand 2000: 284–97.

63   P. Spencer 1997–2016; N. Spencer, Stevens, and Binder 2014.

64   On this being the correct reading, rather than the usual Year 11, see Van Dijk 2011.

65   Brand 2000: 283.

66   These reliefs are published in Epigraphic Survey 1985, with a commentary provided in Murnane 1990, which provides the underpinning for the rest of this section.

67   Kitchen 1968–90: I, 33–35[13, 14], 1993–2014: I, 26–28[13, 14]; 1993–99: I, 36–39[13, 14]).

68   See Dodson 2014a: 76–81, 135–38 and 2018: 53–60 for a discussion of Egyptian foreign affairs during this period; for a translation of the Amarna Letters see Moran 1992.

69   A debate continues on whether the events to be related should indeed be dated to the death of Tutankhamun, or to the death of Akhenaten a decade earlier. For arguments in favor of the later dating, see Dodson 2018: 89–94.

70   See Murnane 1990: 25–29.

71   Rockefeller S.884 (Kitchen 1968–90: I, 11–12[2]; 1993–2014: I, 9–10[2]; 1993–99: I, 17–19[2]); a badly damaged second stela from the same site (Rockefeller S.885A/b) presumably commemorates the same campaign (Kitchen 1968–90: I, 15–16[4]; 1993–2014: I, 12–13[4]; 1993–99: I, 20–21[2]).

72   Istanbul 10942 (Kitchen 1968–90: I, 17[5]; 1993–2014: I, 14[5]; 1993–99: I, 21–22[5]).

73   Beirut Museum (Kitchen 1968–90: I, 117[56]; 1993–2014: I, 98–99[56]; 1993–99: I, 96[56]).

74   Rockefeller S.885 (Kitchen 1968–90: I, 15–16[4]).

75   Aleppo Museum 384 (Kitchen 1968–90: I, 25[9]; 1993–99: I, 20[9]; 1993–99: I, 26[9]).

76   Brand 2000: 121.

77   B.G. Davies 2013–14: IV, 4–13.

78   The latter is now Brooklyn 39.434 (Kitchen 1968–90: I, 104–06; VII, 8–11).

79   See Murnane 1990: 100 n.12.

80   Kitchen 1968–90: I, 283–301.

81   Helck 1958: 311.

82   Kitchen 1993–99: I, 188–89.

83   Rollin 213 (see n. 34).

84   Kitchen 1968–90: III, 1–36[I.1]; 1993–2014: III, 1–25[I.1]; B.G. Davies 2013–14: III, 1–27.

85   Cairo JE43591, from his lost tomb (Kitchen 1968–90: I, 403[B.VIII.1]; 1993–2014: I, 333[B.VIII.1]; 1993–99: I, 269–97[B.VIII.1].

86   Kitchen 1968–90: I, 306–25[VIII–XI]; 1993–2014: I, 249–63[VIII–XI]; 1993–99: I, 203–17[VIII–XI].

87   Brand 2000: 125–27.

88   Munich Gl. WAF38 (Kitchen 1968 90: III, 295–99[XV.4.5]; 1993–2014: III, 213–15[XV.4.5]; B.G. Davies 2013–14: III, 243–44[XV.4.5]).

Notes to Chapter 3

1   Brand 2000: 302–305.

2   Brand 2000: 301–302.

3   See Brand 2000: 305–309 for arguments against earlier proposals for a significantly longer reign for the king, adjusted in light of the correction of the year on the Gebel Barkal stela from 11 to 9 (see n. 64).

4   Aston 2012–13: 295; but cf. Dodson 2018: 130–32 for the issues surrounding the use of this kind of data.

5   For an overview of Egyptian tombs and their development over time, see Dodson and Ikram 2008.

6   For a survey of royal funerary monuments over time, see Dodson 2016c.

7   On this identification of the tomb of Amenhotep I, with previous discussions, see Dodson 2013.

8   Porter and Moss 1972: 407–21; Osing 1977; Brand 2000: 228–49; Stadelmann 2015.

9   Hölscher 1939: 81–82.

10   Martinez 2007; 2008.

11   Martinez feels it "difficult to assign these traces to the time of Rameses I" (2007: 46), preferring to assign the original temple to the mid-Eighteenth Dynasty. However, he gives no substantive reason for excluding Rameses I, and all mid-Eighteenth Dynasty kings have known memorial temples.

12   See detailed analysis in Brand 2000: 238–44, in particular his refutation of claims that the vestibule was decorated jointly by Rameses II and Sethy I during some kind of coregency (cf. pages 34–35).

13   For the debate on the original burial place of Thutmose I, see the summary in Roehrig 2016: 185–86, with references.

14   For all these compositions, see Hornung 1999.

15   Cf. Dodson 2018: 120.

16   Porter and Moss 1960–64: 535–45; Thomas 1966: 104–7; Reeves 1990: 92–94; Donadoni 1966; Hornung 1991; Brand 2000: 256–59; Weeks (ed.) 2000: 21; Weeks (ed.) 2001: 194–211.

17   Roehrig 1995: 90–92.

18   Thomas 1978; Weeks 2016: 106–107.

19   Brand 2000: 257.

20   Weeks 2016.

21   Complete examples were found in the tomb of Tutankhamun, with fragments in those of Thutmose IV and Amenhotep III.

22   Belzoni 1820: 237.

23   Hawass and el Awady 2016.

24   Romer 1981: 75–78.

25   For these, see Dodson 2016d: 245–53.

26   Not a single fragment of such a thing has ever come to light and, as this is also true for Rameses II, it appears certain that neither king had one, given that substantive remains survive from all other New Kingdom kings known to have had a proper burial—even when, as in the case of Akhenaten, his sarcophagus had been purposely broken up as part of an attempt to destroy both his memory and his afterlife.

27   As attested by the intact set of Tutankhamun (Porter and Moss 1960–64: 572), the stripped examples of Thutmose I and III (Porter and Moss 1960–64: 662[2], 660[14]), and fragments of one of Amenhotep III (Yoshimura and Kondo 1995: 18).

28   Soane Museum M470 (Porter and Moss 1960–64: 543; J.H. Taylor 2017); for the definition of "coffin" as an anthropoid container irrespective of material, and a "sarcophagus" as a rectangular outer one, again irrespective of material, see Ikram and Dodson 1998: 193, 244.

29   Cf. the decoration of some New Kingdom private burial chambers essentially as "inside-out sarcophagi" (e.g. TT201 [Re – S. & D. Redford 1994: 15–20]).

30   Porter and Moss 1960–64: 557, 562–63, 4.

31   See Hayes 1935.

32   Damarany and Cahail 2017.

33   Porter and Moss 1960–64: 555.

34   Dodson 1994; 2016e.

35   For example, some found at Medinet Habu, probably moved there when the king's mummy was taken there for restoration (Hölscher 1954: 5, 10 n.48).

36   Examples were deposited along with the burials of Apis bulls at Saqqara, and others were found at Abydos.

37   Bovot 1998; 2003: 80–168.

38   For these, see Reeves 1990: 91, 99 n.5; Romer 1981: 65–66.

39   Ikram 1995: 237–96.

Notes to Chapter 4

1   For the last years of the Nineteenth Dynasty, see Dodson 2016a.

2   Redford 2002; Hawass et al. 2012.

3   For the last years of the Twentieth Dynasty and the beginning of the Twenty-first, see Dodson 2012: 3–38.

4   Porter and Moss 1960–64: 661; Kitchen 1968–90: VI, 838; 1993–2014: VI, 573; Ritner 2009: 99–100[19].

5   Where some of Sethy's *shabti*s were found: see n. 35.

6   Jansen-Winkeln 2007: 22–23[3.36]; Ritner 2009: 115.

7   Jansen-Winkeln 2007: 79[6.12].

8   Jansen-Winkeln 2007: 79[6.11]; it is unclear whether another bandage, manufactured in Year 10 of Nesibanebdjed I (a decade and a half earlier), was an old one used during this restoration or reflects yet another episode of repair work on the mummy.

9   On the history of the Twenty-first Dynasty, see Dodson 2012: 39–82.

10   Jansen-Winkeln 2007: 114–16[9.15A]; Ritner 2009: 158–59.

11   Jansen-Winkeln 2007: 116–17[9.15B]; Ritner 2009: 159.

12   Amenhotep I's burial had been "repeated" in Year 6 of Nesibanebdjed I, but it is unknown whether he had then been returned to his tomb or moved elsewhere before being shifted to Inhapi's sepulcher.

13   See Aston 2013; 2015.

14   The mummy of Panedjem's son-in-law (?) Djedptahiufankh had bandages dated to Shoshenq's Year 11, while that of Panedjem's daughter (and perhaps Djedptahiufankh's wife) Nesitanebetashru included a bandage with an unattributed Year 13.

15   On the chronology of the movements of the royal mummies and their final deposition, see Reeves 1990, superseding all earlier treatments.

Notes to Chapter 5

1   Waddell 1940: 120–21, 128–29, 148–53.

2   Until recently, he was identified with Shabataka, but the relative order of Shabaka and Shabataka has now been reversed, placing the former as Sennacherib's contemporary (see Broekman 2015).

3   On *Sethos* and its influence, see Macpherson 2004.

4   Iversen 1968: 65–75.

5   Benaissa 2013.

6   For the obelisk and its history, see Iversen 1968: 128–41.

7   See Iversen 1961.

8   Works on Belzoni are numerous; for a summary of his career and a bibliography, see Bierbrier (ed.) 2012: 52–53; his most substantial biographies are Mayes 1959 and Hume 2011.

9   Bierbrier 2012: 484–85.

10   Schaden 1979.

11   Belzoni 1820: 230–33.

12   Belzoni 1820: 233–37.

13   Bierbrier 2012: 340–41.

14   Bierbrier 2012: 161–62.

15   Bierbrier 2012: 464; Salvoldi 2018.

16   On Ricci and his relationship with Belzoni, see Salvoldi 2011.

17   Belzoni 1820: 294.

18   Jones 2003: 258–59.

19   Bierbrier 2012: 38–39.

20   Belzoni 1820: 370–71.

21   Only one part survived in the 1880s; otherwise, all that remains are Bicci-derived copies.

22   Bierbrier 2012: 246–47.

23   This effect is also to be seen in the temple at Beit el-Wali, from which extensive casts were taken by Hay (now in the British Museum).

24   Belzoni 1820: 372.

25   On the sarcophagus lid of Rameses III (now Fitzwilliam E.1.1823) and its later history, see Wilson 2002, who, however, and like most other modern writers, confuses the piece with a "sarcophagus lid" gifted by Drovetti to Belzoni when the latter first came to Thebes. In fact, the "Drovetti-lid" was that of the stone coffin of Viceroy of Nubia Setau (BM EA78), from TT289 on Dra Abu'l-Naga; it was removed by Belzoni in early 1817 and joined Salt's First Collection (see Bickerstaffe 2006). The trough of Setau's coffin is still in the tomb, while the coffer of Rameses III (Louvre D.1) was later removed from KV11 by Salt.

26   Belzoni 1820; it soon went into French (1821) and Italian (1823) editions.

27   On Curtin, see De Keersmaecker 2000; Morkot 2013, 2015.

28   Bierbrier 2012: 594–95.

29   Young 1821a; 1821b.

30   Young 1821b.

31   Young 1821b.

32   Belzoni 1820: 242.

33   For a full listing of the material, see Belzoni 1822.

34   Anon. 1821a.

35   Anon. 1821b.

36   Of the other material on exhibition, it is possible a display of Belzoni-derived items displayed at 10 New Bond Street in Bath from 7–28 October 1822 was based around material from it. However, while it certainly contained two coffined mummies, one wrapped and one unwrapped (which later passed to Bath Royal Literary and Scientific Institution and are now on long-term loan to Bristol Museum & Art Gallery as H5062 and H5074–5), as did the London show, the contemporary description of the wrapped mummy (Belzoni 1822: 9) makes it clear that this was a Roman example akin to BM EA6704 (Dawson and Gray 1968: 33–34[64]), rather than of Twenty-sixth Dynasty date, like the Bath example.

37   On this and the coffin's postpurchase history, see H. Dorey in J.H. Taylor 2017: 80–93.

38   Sharpe and Bonomi 1864; a commentary on the texts, based on this, was published by Paul Pierret (1836–1916) in 1870.

39   Bierbrier 2012: 68.

40   Thompson 2015: 154–59.

41   Dodson, forthcoming.

42   These provided the principal illustrations for J.H. Taylor's 2017 description of the decoration.

43   Sharpe and Bonomi 1864: 4–8.

44   Bierbrier 2012: 575–76.

45   A police report produced during her later residence in Brussels gives her maiden name as "Banne"; however, a "declaration of intent to marry" lodged by a Giovanni Belzon (sic) with the vicar general's office in London on 12 April 1804 gives his fiancée's name as Sarah Parker Brown (with an age [21] consistent with the known date of birth of Sarah Belzoni) (see J.J. Taylor and Baghiani 2018).

46   For Sarah's career in Brussels, see Warmenbol 2017.

47   These included one of the coffins of the scribe of the Tomb Butehamun, and the Roman mummy it by then contained, sold to the Musées royaux d'Art et Histoire in Brussels in 1847 (E.5299 and E.5288, respectively).

48   Hamill and Mollier 2003: 212–13.

49   Weisse 1880: 36–46.

50   Weisse 1880: 63–66.

51   Weisse 1880: 46–47.

52 The association of Rameses with the monument is owing to Weisse's reliance on the Egyptological advice of Gustav Seyffarth (1796–1885), a philological opponent of Champollion (Bierbrier 2012: 504–505), whose unique method of decipherment saw Rameses as sharing his father's prenomen during Sethy's reign (regarding Sethy I and Rameses II having "reigned jointly for over fifty years"; see Weisse 1880: 48–49, 60).

53 On the broader topic of "Egyptian Mysteries" in Western culture, see Hornung 2001.

54 On her death and the fate of her possessions, see Dodson and Baghiani 2013; Dodson 2016b. It is unclear how Belzoni's gold medallion, apparently in Sarah's possession at her death, passed to the British Museum in 1872 through one Frederick William Collard, who styled himself a descendant of Belzoni (personal communication with Peter Clayton, January 20, 2018); the name 'Collard' seems unknown in the Tucker family.

55 Bierbrier 2012: 114–15.

56 Hartleben (ed.) 1909: 283, 299, 365.

57 Bierbrier 2012: 473.

58 Thompson 2015: 165–70.

59 Ridley 1991.

60 Bierbrier 2012: 96–97.

61 For this episode, see Hartleben (ed.) 1909: 408; Mayes 1959: 239; Thompson 2015: 169. Florence also received a fragment that seems to have come from the exit from chamber I (Florence 2469).

62 Bierbrier 2012: 579–80.

63 Bierbrier 2012: 527.

64 Bierbrier 2012: 325–26.

65 Thompson 2015: 198–207.

66 Lepsius 1853: 418–20.

67 Bierbrier 2012: 355–57.

68 For the story of the discovery of TT320 and a discussion of the many issues involved, see Bickerstaffe 2010.

69 Bierbrier 2012: 83–84.

70 Bierbrier 2012: 288.

71 Bierbrier 2012: 359–61.

72 Bierbrier 2012: 75–76.

73 Bierbrier 2012: 273.

74 Bierbrier 2012: 197.

75 Bierbrier 2012: 223.

76 Maspero 1886: 333 (translated from the French by the author).

77 For the modern history of the royal mummies, see Ikram 2017.

78 Which lay in what is now the parkland just south of the Ministry of Foreign Affairs.

79 Riggs 2014: 199.

80 Bierbrier 2012: 515–16.

81 Sethy I's mummy is covered in Smith 1912: 57–59.

82 Coury 1992.

83 Harris and Weeks 1973: 43, 152–53; Harris and Wente (eds) 1980: 171.

84 Harris and Wente (eds) 1980: 333.

85 Harris and Wente (eds) 1980: 188–212.

86 Among the royal mummies, Thutmose III, who reigned for 54 years, was assessed as "35–40" at death, with a considerable number of others given ages that would have meant accession at, or within a year or two of, birth (cf. Robins 1981). That the problem concerns not just ancient Egyptian remains has been made clear by studies carried out on over a thousand sets of eighteenth–nineteenth-century AD human remains recovered from the crypts of Christ Church, Spitalfields, in London (Reeve and Adams 1993). Of these, nearly half were of individuals whose age at death was indicated by coffin plates. The work concluded that "there was a systematic error which depended on the age of the individual, those under 40 being over-aged, those over seventy being under-aged . . . . Less than 30 percent of the sample were correctly aged—i.e., to within five years of the real age; but 50 percent were assessed to within ten years, and three-quarters to within fifteen years of the correct age." (Molleson and Cox 1993: 169). Among cases of under-aging, individuals who were known certainly to have

died in their late eighties, or nineties, appeared according to the anatomical criteria to be in their sixties, or in one case late fifties!

87   Hawass and Saleem 2016: 151–60.
88   Bierbrier 2012: 318.
89   Bierbrier 2012: 338–39.
90   Bierbrier 2012: 393–94.
91   Bierbrier 2012: 427–28.
92   Murray 1904.
93   Bierbrier 2012: 398–400.
94   Bierbrier 2012: 198–99.
95   Bierbrier 2012: 470.
96   Bierbrier 2012: 101.
97   Bierbrier 2012: 82.
98   Bierbrier 2012: 105–106
99   Carter 1905: 112–15.
100   Bierbrier 2012: 96.
101   Most of these were ultimately published in Hornung 1991.
102   For this and the following, see Hawass and el Awady 2016.
103   Jones 2003.
104   Hawass and el Awady 2016.
105   Factum Arte 2002.
106   Factum Foundation 2017.
107   Factum Foundation 2017: 52–55.

BIBLIOGRAPHY

Abbreviations for periodicals

Ä&L   *Ägypten und Levante: Zeitschrift für ägyptische Archäologie und deren Nachbargebiete* (Vienna: Verlag der Österreichischen Akademie der Wissenschaften).

AncEg   *Ancient Egypt* (Manchester: Ancient Egypt Magazine).

ASAE   *Annales du Service des Antiquités de l'Égypte* (Cairo: Institut Français d'Archéologie Orientale / Supreme Council of Antiquities Press).

BES   *Bulletin of the Egyptological Seminar* (New York: Egyptological Seminar of New York).

BIFAO   *Bulletin de l'Institut Français d'Archéologie Orientale du Caire* (Cairo: Institut Français d'Archéologie Orientale).

CdE   *Chronique d'Egypte* (Brussels: Fondation égyptologique Reine Elisabeth).

EAO   *Égypte Afrique et Orient* (Avignon: Centre d'égyptologie d'Avignon).

EgArch   *Egyptian Archaeology: Bulletin of the Egypt Exploration Society* (London: Egypt Exploration Society).

GM   *Göttinger Miszellen* (Göttingen: Universität Göttingen. Ägyptologisches Seminar).

JARCE   *Journal of the American Research Center in Egypt* (New York: American Research Center in Egypt).

JEA   *Journal of Egyptian Archaeology* (London: Egypt Exploration Fund/Society).

JNES   *Journal of Near Eastern Studies* (Chicago: Chicago University Press).

JSSEA   *Journal of the Society for the Study of Egyptian Antiquities* (Toronto: Society for the Study of Egyptian Antiquities).

Kmt   *Kmt: A Modern Journal of Ancient Egypt* (San Francisco, &c: Kmt Communications).

MMJ   *Metropolitan Museum Journal* (New York: Metropolitan Museum of Art).

MDAIK   *Mitteilungen des Deutschen Archäologischen Instituts, Kairo* (Mainz: Philipp von Zabern).

S&N   *Sudan & Nubia* (London: Sudan Archaeological Research Society).

SAK   *Studien zur altägyptschen Kultur* (Hamburg: H. Buske Verlag).

TSBA   *Transactions of the Society of Biblical Archaeology* (London: Society of Biblical Archaeology).

ZPE   *Zeitschrift für Papyrologie und Epigraphik* (Cologne: Universität zu Köln).

Works cited

Anon. 1821a. "Egyptian Antiquities." *Literary Gazette* 5/223: 268.

Anon. 1821b. "Varieties, Great Britain." *New Monthly Magazine* NS 3: 286.

Aston, D.A. 2012–13. "Radiocarbon, Wine Jars and New Kingdom Chronology." *Ä&L* 22–23: 289–315.

———. 2013. "TT 320 and the ḳ3y of Queen Inhapi – A Reconsideration Based on Ceramic Evidence." *GM 236: 7–20.*

———. 2015. "TT 358, TT 320, and KV 39. Three Early Eighteenth Dynasty Queen's Tombs in the Vicinity of Deir el-Bahari." In *Deir el-Bahari Studies: Special Studies*, edited by Z. Szafranski, 14–42. Warsaw: Polish Centre of Mediterranean Archaeology.

Badawy, A. 1972. "A Monumental Gateway for a Temple of King Sety I: An Ancient Model Restored." In *Miscellanea Wilbouriana*, 1, edited by [B.V. Bothmer], 1–20. Brooklyn: Brooklyn Museum.

Belzoni, G. 1820. *Narrative of the Operations and Recent Discoveries within the Pyramids, Temples, Tombs and Excavations in Egypt and Nubia.* London: John Murray.

———. 1821. *Description of the Egyptian Tomb, Discovered by G. Belzoni.* London: John Murray.

———. 1822. *Catalogue of the Various Articles of Antiquity, to be Disposed of, at the Egyptian Tomb, by Auction, or by Private Contract.* London: William Clowes.

Benaissa, A. 2013. "Ammianus Marcellinus 'Res Gestae' 17.4.17 and the Translator of the Obelisk in Rome's 'Circus Maximus.'" *ZPE* 186: 114–18.

Bickerstaffe, D. 2006. "Strong Man—Wrong Tomb: The Problem of Belzoni's Sarcophagi." *AncEg* 6/6: 22–30.

———. 2010. "The History of the Discovery of the Cache." In *The Royal Cache TT 320: A Re-examination*, edited by E. Graefe and G. Belova, 13–36. Cairo: Supreme Council of Antiquities Press.

Bierbrier, M.L. (ed.) 2012. *Who Was Who in Egyptology*, 4th edition. London: Egypt Exploration Society.

Bovot, J.-L. 1998. "Sethy Ier: le pharaon aux mille et un chaouabtis." *EAO* 11: 37–42.

———. 2003. *Les serviteurs funéraires royaux et princiers de l'Ancienne Égypte.* Paris: Réunion des musées nationaux.

Brand, P.J. 1999. "Secondary Restorations in the Post-Amarna Period." *JARCE* 36: 113–34.

———. 2000. *The Monuments of Seti I: Epigraphic, Historical, and Art Historical Analysis.* Leiden: Brill.

Broekman, G.P.F. 2015. "The Order of Succession between Shabaka and Shabataka; A Different View on the Chronology of the Twenty-fifth Dynasty." *GM* 245: 17–31.

Budge, E.A.W. 1908. *An Account of the Sarcophagus of Seti I, King of Egypt, B.C. 1370.* London: British Museum / Sir John Soane's Museum.

Bunbury, J.M., A. Graham, and M.A. Hunter. 2008. "Stratigraphic Landscape Analysis: Charting the Holocene Movements of the Nile at Karnak through Ancient Egyptian Time." *Geoarchaeology: an International Journal* 23/3: 351–73.

Calverley, A.M. and M.F. Broome. 1933–58. *The Temple of King Sethos I at Abydos*, 4vv. London: Egypt Exploration Society/Chicago: University of Chicago Press.

Carter, H. 1905. "Report of Work Done in Upper Egypt (1903–1904)." *ASAE* 6: 112–29.

Caulfield, A. St G. 1902. *The Temple of the Kings at Abydos (Sety I.).* London: Bernard Quaritch.

Champollion, J.-F. 1824. *Precis du système hiéroglyphique des anciens Égyptiens.* Paris: Treuttel & Wurtz.

Coury, R.M. 1992. "The Politics of the Funereal: The Tomb of Saad Zaghlul." *JARCE* 29: 191–200.

Cruz-Uribe, E. 1978. "The Father of Ramses I: OI 11456." *JNES* 37: 237–44.

Damarany, A. and K.M. Cahail. 2017. "The Sarcophagus of the High Priest of Amun, Menkheperre, from the Coptic Monastery of Apa Moses at Abydos." *MDAIK* 72: 11–30.

David, R. 2016. *Temple Ritual at Abydos.* London: Egypt Exploration Society.

Davies, B.G. 2013–14. *Ramesside Inscriptions: Translated and Annotated. Notes and Comments*, III–IV. Chichester: Wiley Blackwell.

Davies, W.V. 2001. "Kurgus 2000: The Ancient Egyptian Inscriptions." *S&N* 5: 46–58.

Dawson, W.R. and P.H.K. Gray. 1968. *Catalogue of Egyptian Antiquities in the British Museum, I: Mummies and Human Remains.* London: Trustees of the British Museum.

De Keersmaecker, R. 2000. "… My Irish Lad." *ASTENE Bulletin* 10: 21–22.

Delia, R.D. 1979. "A New Look at Some Old Dates: A Reexamination of Twelfth Dynasty Double Dated Inscriptions." *BES* 1: 15–28.

———. 1982. "Doubts about Double Dates and Coregencies." *BES* 4: 55–69.

Delvaux, L. 1992. "Amenhotep, Horemheb et Paramessou: Les grandes statues de scribes à la fin de la 18ᵉ dynastie." In *L'atelier de l'orfèvre: mélanges offerts à Ph. Derchain*, edited by M. Broze and P. Talon, 47–53. Leuven: Peeters.

Dodson, A. 1990. "Crown Prince Djhutmose and the Royal Sons of the Eighteenth Dynasty." *JEA* 76: 87–96.

———. 1994. *The Canopic Equipment of the Kings of Egypt*, with contributions by O.J. Schaden, E.C. Brock, and M. Collier. London: Kegan Paul International.

———. 1997/98. "The So-Called Tomb of Osiris at Abydos." *Kmt* 8/4: 37–47.

———. 2005. "Bull Cults." In *Divine Creatures: Animal Mummies in Ancient Egypt*, edited by S. Ikram, 72–105. Cairo: American University in Cairo Press.

———. 2010. "The Burials of Ahmose I." In *Thebes and Beyond: Studies in Honour of Kent R. Weeks*, edited by Z. Hawass and S. Ikram, 25–33. Cairo: Conseil Suprême des Antiquités.

———. 2012. *Afterglow of Empire: Egypt from the Fall of the New Kingdom to the Saite Renaissance.* Cairo: American University in Cairo Press.

———. 2013. "On the Burials and Reburials of Ahmose I and Amenhotep I." *GM* 238: 19–24.

———. 2014a. *Amarna Sunrise: Egypt from Golden Age to Age of Heresy.* Cairo: American University in Cairo Press.

———. 2014b. "The Coregency Conundrum." *Kmt* 25/2: 28–35.

———. 2016a. *Poisoned Legacy: The Fall of the Nineteenth Egyptian Dynasty*, paperback edition. Cairo: American University in Cairo Press.

———. 2016b. "The Death of Amelia Edwards – and the grave of Belzoni's god-daughter." *ASTENE Bulletin* 67: 20.

———. 2016c. *The Royal Tombs of Ancient Egypt.* Barnsley: Pen & Sword.

———. 2016d. "Sarcophagi." In *The Oxford Handbook of the Valley of the Kings*, edited by R.H. Wilkinson and K. Weeks, 245–59. Oxford: Oxford University Press.

———. 2016e. "Canopics." In *The Oxford Handbook of the Valley of the Kings*, edited by R.H. Wilkinson and K. Weeks, 260–67. Oxford: Oxford University Press.

———. 2018. *Amarna Sunset: Nefertiti, Tutankhamun, Ay, Horemheb, and the Egyptian Counter-Reformation*, revised edition. Cairo: American University in Cairo Press.

———. Forthcoming. "The British Isles." In *A History of Egyptology*, edited by A. Bednarski, A. Dodson, and S. Ikram. Cambridge: Cambridge University Press.

Dodson, A. and A. Baghiani 2013. "Restoration of the Headstone of Sarah Belzoni in the Mont à l'Abbé Cemetery, St Helier, Jersey." *ASTENE Bulletin* 55: 14.

Dodson, A. and D. Hilton. 2010. *The Complete Royal Families of Ancient Egypt*, paperback edition. London: Thames & Hudson.

Dodson, A. and S. Ikram. 2008. *The Tomb in Ancient Egypt: Royal and Private Sepulchres from the Early Dynastic Period to the Romans.* London & New York: Thames & Hudson / Cairo: American University in Cairo Press.

Donadoni, S. 1966. *La decorazione della tomba di Seti I nella Valle dei Re.* Milan: Fratelli Fabbri.

Dorman, P.F. 1988. *The Monuments of Senenmut: Problems in Historical Methodology.* London: Kegan Paul International.

Epigraphic Survey 1986. *Reliefs and Inscriptions at Karnak, 4: The Battle Reliefs of King Sety I.* Chicago: Oriental Institute.

Factum Arte 2002. *The Tomb of Seti I: Digital Technology in Conservation / La Tumba de Seti I: tecnología digital para la conservación.* London & Madrid: Factum Arte, http://www.factumarte.com/resources/files/ff/publications_PDF/SETI_Report_2002.pdf

Factum Foundation. 2017. *Two Hundred Years in the Life of the Tomb of Seti I: Changing Attitudes to Preservation and the Role of Non-contact Recording in the Production of Facsimiles for Heritage Management from the C19th to the C21st.* London: Factum Foundation, http://www.factumarte.com/resources/files/ff/publications_PDF/17p0006_w_pamphlet_all_withcover.pdf

Frankfort, H. 1926. "Preliminary Report of the Expedition to Abydos 1925–6." *JEA* 12: 157–65.

———. 1933. *The Cenotaph of Seti I at Abydos.* London: Egypt Exploration Society.

Gaballa, G.A. and K.A. Kitchen, 1968. "Ramesside Varia I." *CdE* 43/86: 259–70.

Gaber, A. 2013. "Aspects of the Deification of Sety I." *Cahiers de Karnak* 14: 337–82.

Goedicke, H. 1981. "The '400-Year Stela' Reconsidered." *BES* 3: 25–42.

Griffith, F.Ll. 1927. "The Abydos Decree of Seti I at Nauri." *JEA* 13: 193–208.

Habachi, L. 1977. *The Obelisks of Egypt: Skyscrapers of the Past.* New York: Charles Scribner's Sons.

Hamill, J. and P. Mollier. 2003. "Rebuilding the Sanctuaries of Memphis: Egypt in Masonic Iconography and Architecture." In *Imhotep Today: Egyptianizing Architecture*, edited by J.-M. Humbert and C. Price, 207–20. London: UCL Press.

Harris, J.E. and K.R. Weeks. 1973. *X-Raying the Pharaohs.* London: Macdonald.

Harris, J.E. and E.F. Wente (eds). 1980. *An X-Ray Atlas of the Pharaohs.* Chicago: University of Chicago Press.

Hartleben, H. (ed.). 1909. *Lettres et journaux de Champollion*, II: *lettres et journaux écrits pendant le voyage d'Égypte.* Paris: Ernest Leroux.

Hawass, Z. and T. el Awady 2016. "The Tunnel Inside the Tomb of Seti I (KV 17): The Work of the Egyptian Mission, 2007–2010." In *Valley of the Kings since Howard Carter: Proceedings of the Luxor Symposium November 4, 2009*, edited by H. Elleithy, 59–93. Cairo: Ministry of Antiquities.

Hawass, Z., S. Ismail, A. Selim, S.N. Saleem, D. Fathalla, S. Wasef, A.Z. Gad, R. Saad, S. Fares, H. Amer, P. Gostner, Y.Z. Gad, C.M. Pusch, and A.R. Zink. 2012. "Revisiting the Harem Conspiracy and Death of Ramesses III: Anthropological, Forensic, Radiological, and Genetic Study." *British Medical Journal* 345/7888.

Hawass, Z. and S.N. Saleem. 2016. *Scanning the Pharaohs: CT Imaging of the New Kingdom Royal Mummies.* Cairo: American University in Cairo Press.

Hayes, W.C. 1935. *Royal Sarcophagi of the XVIII Dynasty.* Princeton: Princeton University Press.

Helck, W. 1958. *Zur Verwaltung des Mittleren und Neuen Reichs.* Leiden: E.J. Brill.

Hölscher, U. 1939. *The Excavation of Medinet Habu, II: The Temples of the Eighteenth Dynasty.* Chicago: University of Chicago Press.

———. 1954. *The Excavation of Medinet Habu, V: The Post-Ramessid Remains.* Chicago: University of Chicago Press.

Hope, C.A. and R. Ashten. 2017. "The Proscription of Seth Revisited." In *The Cultural Manifestation of Religious Experience: Studies in Honour of Boyo G. Ockinga,* edited by C. Di Biase-Dyson and L. Donovan, 273–83. Münster: Ugarit.

Hornung, E. 1991. *The Tomb of Pharaoh Seti I/Das Grab Sethos' I.* Zürich: Artemis.

———. 1992. "Zum Grab Sethos I. in seinem ursprünglichen Zustand." In *After Tut'ankhamūn: Research and Excavation in the Royal Necropolis at Thebes,* edited by C.N. Reeves, 91–98. London: Kegan Paul International.

———. 1995a. "Frühe Besucher und frühe Zerstörungen im Sethos-Grab." In *Divitiae Aegypti: koptologische und verwandte Studien zu Ehren von Martin Krause,* edited by C. Wietheger-Fluck, L. Langener, S. Richter, S. Schaten, and G. Wurst, 162–67. Wiesbaden: Dr. Ludwig Reichert.

———. 1995b. "Studies on the Decoration of the Tomb of Seti I." In *Valley of the Sun Kings: New Explorations in the Tombs of the Pharaohs,* edited by R.H. Wilkinson, 70–73. Tucson: University of Arizona Egyptian Expedition.

———. 1999. *The Ancient Egyptian Books of the Afterlife,* translated by D. Lorton. Ithaca, NY: Cornell University Press.

———. 2001. *The Secret Lore of Egypt: Its Impact on the West,* translated by D. Lorton. Ithaca, NY: Cornell University Press.

Hume, I.N. 2011. *Belzoni: The Giant Archaeologists Love to Hate.* Charlottesville, VA: University of Virginia Press.

Ikram, S. 1995. *Choice Cuts: Meat Production in Ancient Egypt.* Leuven: Peeters.

———. 2017. "From Thebes to Cairo: the Journey, Study, and Display of Egypt's Royal Mummies, Past, Present and Future." In *Volume in onore di M. Capasso,* edited by P. Davoli, 867–83. Lecce: University of Lecce.

Ikram, S. and A. Dodson. 1998. *The Mummy in Ancient Egypt: Equipping the Dead for Eternity.* London: Thames & Hudson.

Iversen, E. 1961. *The Myth of Egypt and its Hieroglyphs in European Tradition.* Copenhagen: G.E.C. Gad.

———. 1968. Obelisks in *Exile,* vol. I: *The Obelisks of Rome.* Copenhagen: G.E.C. Gad.

Jánosi, P. 2010. "Montuhotep-Nebtawyre and Amenemhat I: Observations on the Early Twelfth Dynasty in Egypt." *MMJ* 45: 7–20.

Jansen-Winkeln, K. 2007. *Inschriften der Spätzeit,* vol. I, *Die 21. Dynastie.* Wiesbaden: Harrassowitz.

Jones, M. 2003. "The Work of the American Research Center in Egypt in the Tomb of Sety I in the Valley of the Kings, 1998–1999." In *Egyptology at the Dawn of the Twenty-first Century: Proceedings of the Eighth International Congress of Egyptologists, Cairo, 2000,* edited by Z. Hawass, 252–61. Cairo: American University in Cairo Press, 2003.

Kitchen, K.A. 1968–90. *Ramesside Inscriptions: Historical and Biographical,* 8vv. Oxford: Blackwell.

———. 1993–2014. *Ramesside Inscriptions: Translated and Annotated. Translations.* Oxford: Blackwell.

———. 1993–99. *Ramesside Inscriptions: Translated and Annotated. Notes and Comments,* vols. I–II. Oxford: Blackwell.

Leblanc, C. 1988. "L'identification de la tombe de Ḥenout-mi-Rê': fille de Ramsès II et grande épouse royale." *BIFAO* 88, 131–46.

———. 1989. *Ta Set Neferou. Une nécropole de Thèbes-Ouest et son histoire,* I: *Géographie - Toponymie historique de l'exploration scientifique du site.* Cairo: Nubar Printing House.

———. 1993/94. "Les sources grecques et les colosses de Ramsès Rê-en-hekaou et de Touy, au Ramesseum." *Memnonia* 4–5: 71–101.

Leblanc, C. and D. Esmoingt. 2014. "Le colosse de Touy, mère de Ramsès II, retrouve sa place dans la première cour du Ramesseum." *Memnonia* 25, 89–105.

Lefébure, E. 1886. *Les hypogées royaux de Thèbes*, vol. I/1–3: *Le tombeau de Séti Ier*. Paris: Ernest Leroux.

Lepsius, R. 1853. *Letters from Egypt, Ethiopia, and the Peninsula of Sinai*, translated by L. and J.B. Horner. London: Henry G. Bohn.

Löhr, B. 1975. "Aḫanjāti in Memphis." *SAK* 2: 139–87.

Macpherson, J. 2004. "The Travels of Sethos." *Lumen* 23: 235–54.

Mahmoud, A. 2011. *Catalogue of the Funerary Objects from the Servant in the Place of Truth Sennedjem*. Cairo: Institut français d'archéologie orientale.

Malek, J. 2012. *Topographical Bibliography of Ancient Egyptian Hieroglyphic Texts, Reliefs and Paintings*, vol. 8/4: *Objects of Provenance Not Known, Stelae (Dynasty XVIII and Roman Period)*. Oxford: Griffith Institute.

Mariette, A. 1857. *Le Sérapeum de Memphis decouvert et décrit par Aug. Mariette. Ouvrage dédié à S A.I. Mgr. le Prince Napoléon et publié sous les auspices de S.E.M. Achille Fould, ministre d'état*. Paris: Gide.

Martin, G.T. 1989. *The Memphite Tomb of Ḥoremḥeb, Commander-in-Chief of Tutʻankhamūn*, vol. I. London: Egypt Exploration Society.

———. 1997. *The Tomb of Tia and Tia. A Royal Monument of the Ramesside Period in the Memphite Necropolis*. London: Egypt Exploration Society.

Martinez, P. 2007. "Seti I and the Ghosts of What Had Been: A Reappraisal of Qurna Temple and its History." *Kmt* 18/1: 36–46.

———. 2008. "Par des portails anépigraphes: un réexamen des développements architecturaux du début de l'époque ramesside à Thèbes Ouest." *CdE* 83: 41–74.

Maspéro, G. 1886. "Procès-verbal de l'ouverture des momies de Seti I et Seqenenra Taâaqen." *American Journal of Archaeology and of the History of the Fine Arts* 2/3: 331–33.

———. 1889. *Les momies royales de Déir el-Bahari*. Cairo: Mission archéologique française.

Maspero, G. and E. Brugsch. 1881–87. *La trouvaille de Deir-el-Bahari*, 2vv. Cairo: Imprimerie française F. Mourès & Co.

Masquelier-Loorius, J. 2013. *Séthi Ier et le début de la XIXe dynastie*. Paris: Pygmalion.

Mayes, S. 1959. *The Great Belzoni*. London: Putnam.

Molleson T. and M. Cox 1993. *The Spitalfields Project*, vol. II: *The Anthropology, The Middling Sort*. York: Council for British Archaeology.

Moran, W.L. 1992. *The Amarna Letters*. Baltimore and London: Johns Hopkins University Press.

Morkot, R. 2013, 2015. "The 'Irish lad' James Curtin, 'servant' to the Belzonis." *ASTENE Bulletin* 56: 16–19; 65: 18.

Murnane, W.J. 1977. *Ancient Egyptian Coregencies*. Chicago: Oriental Institute.

———. 1990. *The Road to Kadesh: A Historical Interpretation of the Battle Reliefs of King Sety I at Karnak*, 2nd edition. Chicago: Oriental Institute.

———. 1991. "In Defense of the Middle Kingdom Double Dates." *BES* 3: 73–82.

Murray, M.A. 1904. *The Osireion at Abydos*. London: Bernard Quaritch.

Nelson, H.H. 1981. *The Great Hypostyle Hall at Karnak*, vol. 1/1: *The Wall Reliefs*. Chicago: Oriental Institute.

Osing, J. 1977. *Der Tempel Sethos' I. in Gurna*, vol. 1: *die Reliefs und Inschriften*. Mainz: Philipp von Zabern.

Pierret, P. 1870. "Le sarcophage de Séti Ier." *Revue archéologique* NS 21: 285–306.

Porter, B. and R.L.B. Moss. 1934. Topographical *Bibliography of Ancient Egyptian Hieroglyphic Texts, Reliefs, and Paintings*, vol. IV: *Lower and Middle Egypt*. Oxford: Clarendon Press.

———. 1939. *Topographical Bibliography of Ancient Egyptian Hieroglyphic Texts, Reliefs, and Paintings*, vol. VI: *Upper Egypt: Chief Temples (excl. Thebes)*. Oxford: Clarendon Press.

———. 1952. *Topographical Bibliography of Ancient Egyptian Hieroglyphic Texts, Reliefs, and Paintings*, vol. VII: *Nubia, Deserts, and Outside Egypt*. Oxford: Clarendon Press/ Griffith Institute.

———. 1960–64. *Topographical Bibliography of Ancient Egyptian Hieroglyphic Texts, Reliefs and Paintings*, vol. I: *The Theban Necropolis*. 2nd edition. Oxford: Clarendon Press/ Griffith Institute.

———. 1972. *Topographical Bibliography of Ancient Egyptian Hieroglyphic Texts, Reliefs and Paintings*, vol. II: *Theban Temples*. 2nd edition. Oxford: Griffith Institute.

———. 1974–81. *Topographical Bibliography of Ancient Egyptian Hieroglyphic Texts, Reliefs and Paintings*, vol. III: *Memphis*. 2nd edition by J. Málek. Oxford: Griffith Institute.

Raven, M.J. and R. van Walsem. 2014. *The Tomb of Meryneith at Saqqara*. Turnhout: Brepols.

Redford, S. 2002. *The Harem Conspiracy: The Murder of Ramesses III*. DeKalb, IL: Northern Illinois University Press.

Redford, S. and D. 1994. *The Tomb of Re'a*. Toronto: Akhenaten Temple Project.

Reeve, J. and M. Adams. 1993. *The Spitalfields Project*, vol. I: *the Archaeology, Across the Styx*. York: Council for British Archaeology.

Reeves, C.N. 1990. *Valley of the Kings: The Decline of a Royal Necropolis*. London: Kegan Paul International.

Ridley, R.T. 1991. "Champollion in the Tomb of Seti I: An Unpublished Letter." *CdE* 66/131–32: 23–30.

Riggs, C. 2014. *Unwrapping Ancient Egypt*. London: Bloomsbury.

Ritner, R.K. 2009. *The Libyan Anarchy: Inscriptions from Egypt's Third Intermediate Period*. Atlanta: Society of Biblical Literature.

Robins, G. 1981. "The Value of the Estimated Ages of the Royal Mummies at Death as Historical Evidence." *GM* 45: 63–68.

Roehrig, C.H. 1995. "Gates to the Underworld: The Appearance of Wooden Doors in the Royal Tombs in the Valley of the Kings." In *Valley of the Sun Kings: New Explorations in the Tombs of the Pharaohs. Papers from the University of Arizona International Conference on the Valley of the Kings*, edited by R.H. Wilkinson, 82–107. Tucson, AZ: University of Arizona Egyptian Expedition.

———. 2016. "Royal Tombs of the Eighteenth Dynasty." In *The Oxford Handbook of the Valley of the Kings*, edited by R.H. Wilkinson and K.R. Weeks, 183–99. New York: Oxford University Press.

Romer, J. 1981. *Valley of the Kings*. London: Michael Joseph and Rainbird.

Salvoldi, D. 2011. "Ricci, Belzoni, Salt and the Works in the Valley of the Kings: New Light from the Ricci Travel Account." In *L'Egitto in età Ramesside: atti del Convegno Chianciano Terme 17–18 dicembre 2009*, edited by D. Picchi, 33–41. Milan: Silvana Editoriale.

———. 2018. *From Siena to Nubia: Alessandro Ricci in Egypt and Sudan, 1817–22*. Cairo: American University in Cairo Press.

Schaden, O.J. 1979. "Preliminary Report on the Re-clearance of Tomb 25 in the Western Valley of the Kings (WV-25)." *ASAE* 63: 161–68.

Sharpe, S. and J. Bonomi. 1864. *The Alabaster Sarcophagus of Oimenepthah I., King of Egypt, Now in Sir John Soane's Museum, Lincoln's Inn Fields*. London: Longman, Green, Longman, Roberts and Green.

Smith, G.E. 1912. *The Royal Mummies*. Cairo: Institut français d'archéologie orientale.

Sourouzian, H. 1983. "Ḥenout-mi-Rê, fille de Ramsès II et grande épouse du roi." *ASAE* 69: 365–71.

Spalinger, A. 2009. *The Great Dedicatory Inscription of Ramesses II: a Solar-Osirian Tractate at Abydos.* Leiden: E.J. Brill.

Spencer, N., A. Stevens, and M. Binder. 2014. *Amara West: Living in Egyptian Nubia.* London: Trustees of the British Museum.

Spencer, P. 1997–2016. *Amara West*, 3vv. London: Egypt Exploration Society.

Stadelmann, R. 2015. "The Temple of Millions of Years of Seti I at Qurna / El Templo de Millones de Años de Seti I en Qurna." In *Los templos de millones de años en Tebas / The temples of millions of years in Thebes*, edited by M. Seco Álvarez and A. Jódar Miñarro, 167–93. Granada: Editorial Universidad de Granada.

Stannish, S.M. forthcoming. "Papyrus Rollin 213 and the Aftermath of the Amarna Period." *JSSEA.*

Taylor, J.H. 2017. *Sir John Soane's Greatest Treasure: The Sarcophagus of Seti I.* London: Pimpernel Press.

Taylor, J.J. and A. Baghiani. 2018. "Belzoni's Marriage." *ASTENE Bulletin* 76: 13–14.

Te Velde, H. 1967. *Seth, God of Confusion: A Study of his Role in Egyptian Mythology and Religion.* Leiden: E.J. Brill.

Thomas, E. 1966. *The Royal Necropoleis of Thebes*, vol. I: *The Major Cemeteries.* Princeton: Privately Printed.

———. 1978. "The 'well' in Kings' Tombs of Biban el-Molûk." *JEA* 64: 80–83.

Thompson, J. 2015. *Wonderful Things: A History of Egyptology*, vol. 1: *From Antiquity to 1881.* Cairo: American University in Cairo Press.

Van Dijk, J. 2011. "The Date of the Gebel Barkal Stela of Seti I." In *Under the Potter's Tree: Studies on Ancient Egypt Presented to Janine Bourriau on the Occasion of Her 70th Birthday*, edited by D. Aston, B. Bader, C. Gallorini, P. Nicholson, & S. Buckingham, 325–32. Leuven: Peeters.

Von Beckerath, J. 1999. *Handbuch der ägyptischen Königsnamen*, 2nd edition. Mainz: Phillip von Zabern.

Waddell, W.G. 1940. *Manetho.* Cambridge, MA: Harvard University Press/London: William Heinemann.

Warmenbol, E. 2017. "Sarah Belzoni and Her Mummy: Notes on the Early History of the Egyptian Collection in Brussels." In *Collections at Risk: New Challenges in a New Environment. Proceedings of the 29th CIPEG Annual Meeting in Brussels, September 25–28, 2012, Royal Museums of Art and History, Brussels, Belgium*, edited by C. Derriks, 149–78. Atlanta, GA: Lockwood Press.

Weeks, K.R. (ed.) 2000. *Atlas of the Valley of the Kings.* Cairo: American University in Cairo Press.

———. 2001. *The Treasures of the Valley of the Kings: Tombs and Temples of the Theban West Bank in Luxor.* Cairo: American University in Cairo Press.

———. 2016. "The Component Parts of KV Royal Tombs." In *The Oxford Handbook of the Valley of the Kings*, edited by R.H. Wilkinson and K. Weeks, 98–116. Oxford: Oxford University Press.

Weisse, J.A. 1880. *The Obelisk and Freemasonry, According to the Discoveries of Belzoni and Commander Gorringe.* New York: J.W. Bouton.

Wilson, P. 2002. "Rameses III, Giovanni Belzoni and the Mysterious Reverend Browne." In *Egypt through the Eyes of Travellers*, edited by P. Starkey and Nadia El Kholy, 45–56. Durham: ASTENE.

Winlock, H.E. 1921. *Bas-reliefs from the Temple of Rameses I at Abydos.* New York: Metropolitan Museum of Art.

———. 1937. *The Temple of Ramesses I at Abydos.* New York: Metropolitan Museum of Art.

Yoshimura, S. and J. Kondo. 1995. "Excavations at the Tomb of Amenophis III." *EgArch* 7: 17–18.

Young, T. 1821a. "An Explanation of Some of the Principal Hieroglyphics, Extracted from the Article Egypt in the Supplement of the Encyclopaedia Britannica; with Additional Notes." In *Narrative of the Operations and Recent Discoveries within the Pyramids, Temples, Tombs, and Excavations in Egypt and Nubia*, 2nd edition, by G. Belzoni, 487–524. London: John Murray.

———. 1821b. "Remarks on Mr. Belzoni's Plates." In *Narrative of the Operations and Recent Discoveries within the Pyramids, Temples, Tombs, and Excavations in Egypt and Nubia*, 2nd edition, by G. Belzoni, 525–33. London: John Murray.

Sources of Images

All images by the author, except as listed below:

8   Courtesy of the Oriental Institute of the University of Chicago.

10   Composite author/© Metropolitan Museum of Art/Winlock 1921: pl. vii viii; 1937: pl. iii.

12   Francis Dzikowski, © and courtesy Theban Mapping Project (10485).

21   © Trustees of the British Museum.

23   Dylan Bickerstaffe.

41   Dyan Hilton.

43   Vanessa Foott.

44   © Metropolitan Museum of Art.

47   Salima Ikram.

51   Dyan Hilton.

54   Dylan Bickerstaffe.

55   Dylan Bickerstaffe.

58   Dyan Hilton.

59   Adapted from Griffith JEA pl. xxxviii-xliii.

61   Dyan Hilton.

63   Elie Posner, © The Israel Museum, Jerusalem.

77   Martin Davies.

79   Giovanni Belzoni/author.

80   Francis Dzikowski, © and courtesy Theban Mapping Project (16243).

81   Francis Dzikowski, © and courtesy Theban Mapping Project (16242) + Alessandro Ricci, courtesy Bristol City Museum & Art Gallery (H4393B).

82   Francis Dzikowski, © and courtesy Theban Mapping Project (15500).

83   Alessandro Ricci, courtesy Bristol City Museum & Art Gallery (Belzoni H4403).

84   Francis Dzikowski, © and courtesy Theban Mapping Project (16233).

85   Francis Dzikowski, © and courtesy Theban Mapping Project (15496).

86   Francis Dzikowski, © and courtesy Theban Mapping Project (15492).

87   Francis Dzikowski, © and courtesy Theban Mapping Project (10068).

88   Harry Burton, courtesy Metropolitan Museum of Art (T1295).

90   Francis Dzikowski, © and courtesy Theban Mapping Project (16223).

91   Francis Dzikowski, © and courtesy Theban Mapping Project (16222).

92   Francis Dzikowski, © and courtesy Theban Mapping Project (16215).

93   Francis Dzikowski, © and courtesy Theban Mapping Project (16213).

94   Francis Dzikowski, © and courtesy Theban Mapping Project (18248).

95   Francis Dzikowski, © and courtesy Theban Mapping Project (16195).

96   Right: after Alessandro Ricci, courtesy Bristol City Museum & Art Gallery (H4458C).

97   Francis Dzikowski, © and courtesy Theban Mapping Project (16178).

98   Francis Dzikowski, © and courtesy Theban Mapping Project (15465).

99   Francis Dzikowski, © and courtesy Theban Mapping Project (15477).

100   Francis Dzikowski, © and courtesy Theban Mapping Project (16196).

101   Francis Dzikowski, © and courtesy Theban Mapping Project (16184).

102   Francis Dzikowski, © and courtesy Theban Mapping Project (16817).

103   © Trustees of Sir John Soane's Museum.

104   Adapted from Bonomi and Sharpe 1864: pl. i.

105   Adapted from Bonomi and Sharpe 1864: pl. i.

INDEX

The names of Egyptian kings are CAPITALIZED.

Abd el-Rassul, (Sheikh) Alı (d. 1987) 154
Abd el-Rassul, Ahmed (d. 1918/19) 144
Abd el-Rassul, Husein 144
Abd el-Rassul, Muhammad (d. 1926) 144
Abu Hamid 55
Abu Simbel 133
Abydos 2, 18, 31–46, 66, 70, 106, 147, 165 n.36;
  chapel of Rameses I 11, 12, 13, 31; King List of
  Rameses II 133; Kom el-Sultan 31, 45; Osireion
  43–45, 104, 150, 151; Portal Temple 45; pyramid
  of Ahmose I 70; temple of Sethy I 10, 18, 23, 24,
  25, 31–43, 54, 57, 58, 69, 77–78, 137, 143, 144,
  151, 157; Umm el-Qaab 31, 43, 44
Ahmes-Nefertiry (wife of AMENHOTEP I; TT320)
  68, 117–18
AHMOSE I 5, 12, 18, 31, 70, 117, 159
AKHENATEN (AMENHOTEP IV) xi, xii, 5–6, 9,
  12, 23, 25, 27, 28, 38, 47, 56, 59, 80, 124, 159,
  162 nn.29, 30, 163 n.69, 164 n.26
Akka 161 Ch.1 n.10
Aksha (Serra West) 36
Alberti, Leone Battista (1404–72) 120
Alexandria 29, 30, 134; University of 149
Amada 27, 56
Amarna *see* Tell el-Amarna
Amarna Letters 59, 163 n.68
Ameneminet (Deir el-Medina workman) 68
AMENEMOPET 160
Amenemopet (Deir el-Medina Scribe of the Tomb,
  TT215) 32
Amenemopet (viceroy of Nubia) 24, 55, 56
AMENHOTEP I 68, 70, 118, 159, 164 n.7, 165 Ch.4
  n.12
AMENHOTEP II 26, 84, 98, 110, 118, 159, 162 n.30
AMENHOTEP III xi, 9, 18, 23, 27, 47, 49, 59, 80,

84, 133, 134, 159, 160 Ch.1 n.10, 162 n.30, 164
  nn.21, 27
AMENHOTEP IV *see* AKHENATEN
AMENMESES 115, 159
American Research Center in Egypt 154
Ammianus Marcellinus (historian) 120
Amqa 59
Amun(-Re) 6, 7, 8, 18, 21, 25, 26, 27, 28, 35, 47, 50,
  52, 53, 54, 56, 61, 62, 63, 68, 69, 71, 72, 73, 74,
  75, 76, 77, 106, 146; high priest of 52, 66, 68,
  116, 118
Amurru 60, 63, 65
Ankhesenamun (Ankhesenpaaten, wife of
  Tutankhamun) 16, 161 Ch.1 n.3
Antikenmuseum, Basel *see* Basel, Antikenmuseum
Antiquities Service of Egypt/Supreme Council of
  Antiquities 144, 145, 146, 151, 154, 156
Anubis 81, 96, 101, 106
Apis 29, 113, 127, 133, 162 n.14, 165 Ch.3 n.36
Ashahebused (Messenger to Every Foreign Land) 68
Assyria 66, 129
Aswan 27, 72; Gebel Gulab 29, 30, 55
Aten 6, 27, 28
Augustus (Roman emperor) 119, 121
Avaris *see* Tell el-Daba
AY 6, 7, 8, 23, 25, 38, 56, 60, 80, 124, 159

Babylon 134, 161 Ch.1 n.10
Baines, John (b. 1946) 151
Bakenkhonsu (high priest of Amun) 68, 69
Baketwernel (wife of Sethy I) 10, 20, 21
Baki (Deir el-Medina Chief Workman, TT298) 52
Bankes, William John (1786–1855) 128, 132, 143
Basel, Antikenmuseum 140, 155, 156
Basel, University 156

Bath 166 n.36

Bay (chancellor, KV13) 115

Bazil, Hervé 145

Beirut, National Museum 163 n.73

Beit el-Wali 24, 162 n.23, 166 n.23

Belmore, Earl of (Somerset Lowry-Corry, 1774–1841) 127

Belzoni, Giovanni Battista (1778–1823) 87, 96, 103, 123–37, 138, 140, 142, 144, 150, 152, 154, 157, 166 nn.25, 36, 45, 167 n.54

Belzoni, Sarah (1783–1870) 137–40, 166 n.45, 167 n.54

Beni Hasan 26, 27

Berlin, Ägyptisches Museum, object ÄM2058 98, 144

Beth Shan 62, 63; First Stela see Jerusalem (East) Rockfeller S.884

British Museum see London, British Museum

Bonomi, Joseph (1796–1878) 137, 142

Book of Amduat 79, 80, 81, 85, 87, 88, 90, 100, 101, 102, 103, 106

Book of Gates 43, 81, 90, 92, 94, 98, 99, 106, 132, 133, 138

Book of the Dead (Going Forth by Day) 21, 44, 106, 107, 112

Book of the Divine Cow 98, 99

Books of the Underworld 79

Bouriant, Urbain (1849–1903) 145, 150

Bristol City Museum & Art Gallery 140, 166 n.36

Brooklyn, Brooklyn Museum, object 49.183

Broome, Myrtle (1888–1978)

Brugsch, Emile (1842–1930)

Brussels 138, 140, 166 nn.45–46; Musées royaux d'Art et Histoire 166 n.47

Bulaq, Museum 144, 145, 147; see also Cairo, Egyptian Museum

Burton, Harry (1879–1940) 153

Burton, James (1788–1862) 143

Cairo 28, 127, 128, 132, 144, 145, 147, 149; Egyptian Museum 147; objects CG751 2; CG927+CG39210 52; CG61019 115; CG61077 145; JE6039 11; JE26213 145; JE43591 165 n.85; JE44861 8; JE44863–4 161

Ch.1 n.5; JE60137 162 n.13; JE60539 161 Ch.1 n.13; JE100012 15; TR 9/12/22/1–14 111; TR 30/10/26/12 6; National Museum of Egyptian Civilization 159

Calverley, Amice (1896–1959) 151

Cambridge University, Fitzwilliam Museum, object E.1.1823 135, 166 n.25

canopic equipment 19, 20, 21, 29, 44, 45, 110, 111, 134, 136

Carter, Howard (1874–1939) 96, 151, 153, 154, 156

Castello, Matteo da (1555–1632) 121

casts 133, 134, 135, 138, 142, 166 n.23

Champollion, Jean-François (1790–1832) 93, 140, 142, 150, 166 n.52

chariot 28, 60, 61, 62, 66, 90

Chicago, University of 171; Oriental Institute Museum object 11456 10, 161 Ch.1 n.8

coffin 21, 79, 104–10, 115–16, 117, 118, 128, 129, 131, 134, 135, 136, 137–38, 142, 145, 147, 156, 164 n.28, 166 nn.25, 36, 37, 47

Coffin Texts 79

Coleridge, Samuel Taylor (1772–1834) 138

Constantine I (Roman emperor) 120

Constantius II (Roman emperor) 120

Curtin, James (1796–1825) 133, 135, 137, 138, 166 n.27

Dal Cataract 56

Deir el-Bahari 24, 70, 71, 72, 117, 118

Deir el-Medina 52, 68, 84

Description de l'Égypte 123

Djedptahiufankh (3rd Prophet of Amun) 165 Ch.4 n.14

Dra Abu'l-Naga 70, 118, 166 n.25

Drovetti, Bernardino (1776–1852) 127, 166 n.25

Edward VII (king of the United Kingdom) 144

Egypt Exploration Fund/Society 150, 151

Egyptian Research Account 151

Elephantine 27, 55, 162 n.24

false door 70, 76

Florence 142, 143; Museo Archeologico objects 2468 93; 2469 167 n.61

Fontana, Domenico (1543–1607) 130–31
Fouquet, Daniel (1850–1914) 145
Frankfort, Henri (1897–1954) 151
freemasonry 119, 138, 139
FUAD I (r. 1917–36) 159

Galilee, Sea of 62
Gaza 60, 63
Gebel Barkal 56, 164 n.3
Gebel Gulab *see* Aswan, Gebel Gulab
Gebel el-Silsila 43, 54–55
Giza 44, 128, 134, 144, 147
Grébaut, Eugène (1846–1915) 146

Hadrian (Roman emperor) 120
Hamed Aga (governor of Qena) 127
Hammath 62
Hanigalbat 66
Hapi 54
Hat (high priest of Osiris) 46
Hathor 71, 92, 96
HATSHEPSUT 24, 26, 27, 38, 71, 74, 79, 104, 159,
    162 n.29
Hawass, Zahi (b. 1947) 156
Hay, Robert (1799–1863) 129, 166
Heldewier, Garnier de 146
Heliopolis 28, 29, 30, 55, 119
Henutmire (daughter of Sethy I) 20, 21, 23, 161–62
    Ch.2 n.11
HERIHOR 51, 116, 160
Hermapion (writer in Greek) 120, 122
Herodotus (historian) 119, 133
Hirenamunpena (Agent) 116
Hittites 1, 2, 6, 19, 59, 60, 64, 65, 66
HOR 89
HOREMHEB 6, 7, 8, 9, 11–14, 19, 23, 24, 47–48,
    52, 56, 60, 73, 80, 84, 88, 90, 92, 110, 111, 113,
    159, 163 n.59
Hormin (Overseer of Harem) 67
HORSIESET I 21
Horus 35, 39, 53, 93, 96, 99, 149; Four Sons of 106,
    110, 111

Inhapi (wife of TAA) 118, 165 Ch.4 n.12
Insinger, Jan (1854–1918) 145
Irem 66, 162 n.23
Isetneferet (wife of Rameses II) 161–62 n.11
Isis 35, 96, 106, 110
Istabl Antar *see* Speos Artemidos
Istanbul, Eski Şark Eserleri Müzesi, object 10942 163
    n.72
Iunmutef-priest 92, 94
Iuny (viceroy of Nubia) 56

Jersey, Channel Islands 139, 140
Jerusalem 134, 161 Ch.1 n.10
Jerusalem (East), Rockefeller Museum, objects S.884
    63, 163 n.71; S.885 163 n.74; S.885A/b 163
    n.71

El-Kab 27
Kadashman-Enlil (king of Babylon) 161 Ch.1 n.10
Kamal, Ahmed Bey (1851–1923) 144–45
KAMOSE 5, 159
Kanais 53
Karnak 2, 7, 8, 13, 18, 24, 26, 27, 47, 49–52, 59, 60,
    65, 66, 70, 72, 120, 121, 137, 157, 162 n.22, 163
    n.51
Kawa 9, 28
KHAEFRE (Khephren) 44, 128
Khaemwaset B 9, 10
Khartoum, Sudan National Museum, object 2690
    161 Ch.1 n.11
Khonsu (god) 62, 73
Khonsu (Deir el-Medina workman) 106
Khor (Syria-Palestine) 60
Kingston Lacy 128
Kom Ombo 55
Kurgus 55
Kurkur Oasis 58

Lefébure, Eugène (1838–1908) 150
Lepsius, Carl Richard (1810–84) 98, 142, 144, 150,
    167 n.66
Libya 64, 66
Litany of Re 79, 85, 93

Liverpool, Earl of (Robert Banks Jenkinson, 1770–1828) 138

London, British Museum 113, 135 36, 137, 143, 144, 166 n.23, 167 n.54; objects EA78 166 n.25; EA855 142; EA1103 26; EA6704 166 n.36; EA8897 112; EA8900 112; EA29948 109; EA33919 112; EA37579 112; Egyptian Hall 130, 132, 134–35; Sir John Soane's Museum 136, 137–38, 140; objects M470 104, 164 n.28; X74 111; Spitalfields, Christ Church 167 n.86

Loret, Victor (1859–1946) 150

Luxor 132, 144, 145; Museum 20; object CG42139=JE36692 51; temple 27, 47, 55

Maat 18, 66, 85, 87

Maihirpri (Fanbearer, KV36) 105

Manetho (historian) 119, 142, 144

Mariette, Auguste (1821–81) 143, 144, 151

Maspero, (Sir) Gaston (1846–1916) 145

Matafian, Thadeos 144–45

Medinet Habu 14, 21, 116, 165 Ch.3 n.35

memorial temple 20, 24, 52, 59, 71, 71–78, 118, 123, 137, 162 n.22

Memphis 6, 27, 29

MENES 23

Menkheperre (high Priest of Amun) 106, 116, 146

MERENPTAH 31, 43, 44, 45, 54, 66, 106, 142, 149, 151, 159

Mery (high priest of Osiris) 46

Meryamun (son of Rameses II) 106

Meryetaten (daughter of Akhenaten) 6

Meryetre (wife of Thutmose III) 104

Merymaat (son of Rameses II) 106

Michigan, University of 149

Mitanni 66

Metropolitan Museum of Art see New York, Metropolitan Museum of Art

Montju 52

Montjuhirkopeshef (son of Rameses IX, KV19) 134

Mozart, Wolfgang Amadeus (1756–91) 119

Muhammad 'Ali (governor of Egypt) 123

Munich, Staatliche Museum Ägyptischer Kunst, objects ÄS443 112; Gl. WAF38 164 n.88

Murray, Margaret (1863–1963) 151

Murshili II (king of the Hittites) 60

Mut 2, 15, 36, 52, 61, 73

Mutnedjmet (wife of Horemheb) 8

Muttuy see Tuy

Nakhtmin (son of Ay) 6, 23

NAKHTNEBEF (NEKTANEBO I) 52

Nauri 57, 58

Naville, Edouard (1844–1926) 151

Nebamun (vizier) 66

Nedjmet (wife of Herihor) 144

NEFERNEFERUATEN 6, 159

Nefersekheru (Overseer of Granaries) 78

Nefertiry (wife of Rameses II) 21, 52, 156, 161–62 Ch.2 n.11

Nefertiti (wife of Akhenaten) 6, 8; see also NEFERNEFERUATEN

Nefertum 38, 40

Neith 110

Nephthys 106, 110

NESIBANEBJED I (SMENDES) 116, 160, 165 Ch.4 nn.8, 12

Nesitanebetashru (daughter of Panedjem II) 165 Ch.4 nn.8, 14

New York, Metropolitan Museum of Art objects 11.155.3c-d 12–13; 26.7.919 45

Nubia 1, 4, 5, 27, 28, 54, 55, 56–58, 63, 66, 115, 133, 163 n.62

Nut 44, 106

obelisk 26, 29, 30, 55, 69, 72, 119, 120–22, 128, 132, 133, 137, 165 Ch.5 n.6

Ombos (Nubt) 9

Opening of the Mouth 7, 8, 10, 92, 94, 95, 101

Osiris 12, 18, 31, 35, 37, 38, 39, 43, 45, 54, 69, 73, 77, 84, 90, 98, 101, 103, 113, 116, 138, 142

Pakhet 27

Palestine 9, 28, 78, 60, 62, 63, 66

PANEDJEM I 116, 160

Panedjem II (high priest of Amun, TT320) 118, 165 Ch.4 n.14

Paramessu (vizier) 8, 9, 11, 12, 161 Ch.1 n.13; see also RAMESES I

Paris 119, 122, 137; Bibliothèque National, object [pRollin] 213 162 n.34, 163 n.83; Boulevard des Italiens 135; Musée du Louvre 135; objects B.7 93, 141, 137; C.213 57; D.1 135, 166 n.25; E.11100 52

PASEBKHANUT (PSUSENNES I) 116, 170

Paser (vizier) 52, 56, 66

Pashedu (Deir el-Medina Chief Workmen, TT3) 52

Peel, Sir Robert (1788–1850) 138

Petrie, Hilda (1871–1956) 151

Philae 128

Pierret, Paul (1836–1916) 166 n.38

Pr-R'mssw see Qantir

Prepayuyotef (Trainee) 116

Psammis/Psammethis/PSAMTIK II 133

Ptah 18, 29, 35, 37, 113; high priest of 23

Ptah-Sokar 38, 40, 98

Punt 72

Pyramid Texts 79

Qadesh 51, 60, 64–65, 66

Qantir *(Pr-R'mssw)* 38

Qasr Ibrim 55

Quban 56

Qurna temple 72–79, 118, 123, 137

Raia (father-in-law of Sethy I) 12, 14

RAMESES I 1, 9, 10–14, 15, 18, 23, 28, 31, 45, 47, 48, 74, 76, 77, 78, 81, 84, 88, 104, 106, 113, 117–18, 134, 142, 159, 164 n.11

RAMESES II 1, 2, 9, 18, 19, 21, 23, 24, 25, 28, 29, 31, 33–34, 35, 38, 39, 40, 43, 45, 46, 50, 51, 52, 53, 55, 56, 61, 65, 66, 68, 69, 73, 74, 77, 78, 98, 106, 110, 116, 117–18, 123, 127, 133, 137, 139, 142, 145, 146, 147, 149, 157, 159, 161–62 Ch.2 n.11, 162 n.30, 164 nn.12, 26, 166–67 n.52

RAMESES III 51, 98, 109, 115, 128, 131, 135, 148, 160, 166 n.25

RAMESES IV 51, 105, 150, 160

RAMESES V 115, 160

RAMESES VI 98, 115, 160

RAMESES VII 115, 160

RAMESES VIII 115, 160

RAMESES IX 115, 128, 160, 161 Ch.2 n.2

RAMESES X 115, 160, 161 Ch.2 n.2

RAMESES XI 20–21, 115, 160, 161 Ch.2 nn.2, 9

Rameses A *see* RAMESES II

Ramesseum 14, 20, 21, 52, 123

Ramose (son of Sethy A) *see* RAMESES I

Re (TT201) 164 n.29

Re-Horakhty 28, 35, 76, 85, 121

Ricci, Alessandro (1792–1834) 87, 98, 128, 131, 132, 133, 150, 156, 165 Ch.5 n.16

rishi (feathered) coffin 106

Rivadavia, Bernardino (1780–1845) 138

Rockefeller, John D. Jr. (1874–1960) 151

Rome 29, 119–22

Rosellini, Ippolito (1800–43) 93, 142, 150

Ruia (mother-in-law of Sethy I) 12, 14

Sadat, Anwar (1918–81) 149

Sala Pasha, General Comte della 146

Salt, Henry (1780–1827) 123, 127, 128, 135, 136, 166 n.25

Saqqara 9, 18, 19, 29, 67, 162 n.14, 163 n.48, 165 Ch.3 n.36

sarcophagus 14, 15, 44, 45, 79, 80, 84, 104–05, 106, 127, 128, 131, 135, 147, 164 nn.26, 28, 166 n.25

Sekhmet 134

Selqet 91, 110

Senenmut (TT353) 98

Sennacherib (king of Assyria) 119, 165 Ch.5 n.2

Sennedjem (Deir el-Medina workman, TT1) 52, 105, 106

Serapeum 39

Serra West *see* Aksha

Sesebi 27

Setau (viceroy of Nubia, TT289) 166 n.25

Seth 9, 11, 15, 18, 30, 62, 142

SETHNAKHTE 109, 115, 160

Sethos (Greek form of Egyptian royal names)

SETHY I *passim*

SETHY II 115, 142, 159

Sethy A (father of Rameses I) 9–10

Sethy C *see* Sethy I

SHABAKA 49, 119, 165 Ch.5 n.2

SHABATAKA 165 Ch.5 n.2

Sharpe, Samuel (1799–1881) 137
Shasu tribes 60–62
SHOSHENQ I 64, 65, 66, 118, 165 Ch.4 n.14
Shuppiluliuma I (king of the Hittites) 59–60
Shuta (envoy) *see* Sethy A
SIAMUN 117, 160
Sidqi, Isma'il (1875–1950) 147
Sieset (Overseer of Granaries) 68
Sinai 68
SIPTAH 115, 159
Sitre-Tia (mother of Sethy I) 10, 11
Sixtus V (pope of Rome) 120–21
Smith, Grafton Elliot (1871–1937) 137
Smithson, James (c.1765–1829) 135
Soane Museum *see* London, Sir John Soane's
    Museum
Soane, (Sir) John (1753–1837) 136, 137–38
Speos Artemidos (Istabl Antar) 26, 27
squeezes 96, 129, 144, 151, 164
Stephenson, General Sir Frederick (1821–1911) 146
Strasbourg, Institut d'Égyptologie 137
Supreme Council of Antiquities *see* Antiquities
    Service of Egypt
Sussex, Duke of (Prince Augustus Frederick, 1773–
    1843) 138
Suty *see* Sethy A
Syria 1, 5, 9, 28, 51, 58, 59, 60, 63, 64, 66, 115, 119

TAA 118, 145, 159
Taemwadjsy (wife of Khaemwaset B) 9
TAWOSRET 115, 159
Tell el-Amarna 6, 23, 28, 103
Tell el-Daba (Avaris) 9, 28
Tell el-Shihab 62
Tell Hebua 15
Terrasson, Jean (1670–1750) 119
Tewfik (khedive of Egypt) 145
Theban Tombs: TT1 (Sennedjem) 52, 105; TT3
    (Pashedu) 52; TT106 (Paser) 68; TT201 (Re)
    164 n.29; TT215 (Amenemopet) 52; TT289
    (Setau) 166 n.25; TT298 (Baki) 52; TT320
    (Ahmes-Nefertiry, Panedjem II) 117, 118, 144,
    154, 167 n.68; TT353 (Senenmut) 98

THUTMOSE I 5, 24, 36, 55, 64, 79, 159, 164 nn.13,
    27
THUTMOSE II 159
THUTMOSE III 1, 5, 17, 24, 36, 47, 55, 79, 80, 84,
    104, 110, 145, 159, 162 nn.29, 30
THUTMOSE IV 120, 159, 164 n.21
Thutmose B (son of Amenhotep III) 9, 23
Tia C (daughter of Sethy I) 18, 19, 161–62 n.11
Tia (mother of Sethy C) *see* Sitre-Tia
Tiberias, Lake 62
titulary, royal 12, 17–18, 31
Tjenry (Overseer of Works) 163 n.48
Tjia (son-in-law of Sethy I) 18, 19
To-Tjay (high priest of Osiris) 46
Tod 27
Tucker, Selina Belzoni (1821–93) 139
Turin, Museo Egizio, object S.6189+6193 68
Turner, J.M.W. (1775–1851) 138
TUTANKHAMUN 2, 6, 7, 8, 9, 12, 23, 25, 27, 59,
    80, 84, 98, 105, 106, 109, 110, 113, 118, 147,
    149, 156, 159, 161 Ch.1 n.3, 162 n.29, 163
    n.69, 164 nn.21, 27
Tuy (Muttuy) (wife of Sethy I) 12, 14, 18, 19, 20, 21,
    22–23, 52

Valley of the Kings 14, 18, 71, 79, 81, 84, 103,
    104, 110, 118, 124, 137, 142, 150, 156; KV2
    (RAMESES IV) 105; KV9 (RAMESES VI)
    98; KV11 (RAMESES III) 128, 166 n.25;
    KV16 (RAMESES I) 14, 15, 84, 117; KV17
    (SETHY I) 18, 71, 84–113, 116, 117, 137, 139,
    156; KV19 (Montjuhirkopeshef) 124; KV20
    (THUTMOSE I/HATSHEPSUT) 79; KV21
    124; WV22 (AMENHOTEP III) 80; WV23
    (AY) 80, 124; WV25 (AMENHOTEP IV[?])
    124; KV34 (THUTMOSE III) 79, 80; KV35
    (AMENHOTEP II) 84, 118; KV36 (Maihirpri)
    105; KV38 (THUTMOSE I) 18, 79; KV42
    (Meryetre) 104; KV46 (Yuya & Tjuiu) 105,
    110; KV57 (HOREMHEB) 80, 111; KV62
    (TUTANKHAMUN) 7, 80
Valley of the Queens 10, 18, 20, 21; QV38
    (Sitre) 10, 20; QV66 (Nefertiry) 21; QV75
    (Henutmire) 20, 21; QV80 (Tuy) 18, 20

Vatican, Museo Gregoriano Egizio, object 22678 23
vizier 8, 9, 10, 11, 21, 52, 66, 68, 116

Wadi Abad *see* Kanais
Wadi Hammamat 53
Washington DC, Smithsonian Institution 135
Weisse, John A. (1810–88) 138–39
Wenennefer (high priest of Osiris) 46
Wepwawetmose (vizier) 52
Weston-super-Mare 139, 140
Wiedemann, Alfred (1856–1936) 137
Wilkinson, Sir Gardner (1797–1875) 143–44, 154

Wilson (neé Tucker), Sarah Ann (1844–1921) 140
Wilson, Charles Edward (b. 1872) 140

Year 400 Stela *see* Cairo, Egyptian Museum, JE60539
Yenoam 61, 62, 63
Young, Thomas (1773–1829) 133, 140
Yuya (father-in-law of Amenhotep III, KV46) 105

Zaghlul, Sa'd (Egyptian prime minister, 1859–1927) 147, 148, 149
Zananza (Hittite prince) 60